Understanding
SALVATION
in Plain English

Gary Crandall

Understanding SALVATION in Plain English
Copyright © 2106 by Gary Crandall

This book may not be reproduced without written consent from the author, except for the case of brief quotations for the purpose of review or comment.

Published by Harvest Publishing,
A ministry of Harvest Baptist Church, Guam.
P.O. Box 23189
170 C Machuate Street
Barrigada, Guam, 96913

All Scripture quotations are taken from the King James Bible. In a few cases, the archaic verb endings have been changed to match current spelling and usage.

Cover Design by Kristen Carruthers.

ISBN: 978-0-9975392-0-2

Printed in U.S.A. by Ingram Spark

Contents

Introduction

1. The Gospel	11
2. The Need for Salvation	25
3. Salvation in Jesus Christ: WHO Jesus Is	37
4. Salvation in Jesus Christ: WHAT Jesus Did	55
5. Receiving Salvation: Repent and Believe	79
6. Faith and Works	99
7. Assurance of Salvation	122
8. Salvation Words: Born Again, Adoption, Election	145
9. Salvation Words: Redemption, Propitiation, Justification	167
10. Salvation Words: Salvation, Sanctification, Glorification	183

ACKNOWLEDGMENTS

In God's great wisdom, grace, and perhaps a sprinkling of humor, He designed His Church to be interdependent. He means for us to depend upon one another. That is how both the Christian life and church life work. I, for one, rejoice in God's plan for our mutual dependence, for it has been a constant source of encouragement, blessing, ministry, and instruction. God has placed into my life numerous beloved believers. These men and women of God have used their spiritual gifts and God-given abilities to make this book possible. My spiritual mentor, teacher, and long-time friend, Dr. John C. Whitcomb, taught me by life and example the value of teaching the deep truths of God in understandable ways, and to use "the only book God ever wrote" as the all-sufficient text.

Dr. Marty Herron, pastor of Harvest Baptist Church, along with Dr. Bobby Wood, incubated the idea for the book until it hatched full blown into my heart. Pastor Jared Baldwin provided a constant flow of encouragement, oversight, helpful suggestions, and gallons of coffee and tea. Miss Abigail Thompson corrected the manuscript with unusual deft and tact. Fellow teachers at Harvest Baptist Bible College offered helpful suggestions, input, and prayer. More than two dozen of my Micronesian students read portions of the manuscript and pointed out words and ideas which required change or explanation. Christy Marshall cheerfully provided much needed help with graphics. Kristen Carruthers expertly created the cover and formatted the text. And most of all, my dear wife, Sherrie, for her unfailing love and support, her help when I was stuck, and her kindness always. To all these and more, I am deeply grateful.

Introduction

"What must I do to be saved?" asked the Philippian jailer, whose story is recorded in the Bible (Acts 16:30). That same question is asked by many people today. As we have traveled to a number of islands and talked with pastors, missionaries and people in the villages, it has become evident that there is much confusion about salvation. Because our eternal destiny depends on having the right answer, we need to seriously consider this most important question. Thankfully, the Bible gives a very clear and direct response to this question of *"What must I do to be saved?"* The Apostle Paul answered this way: *"Believe on the Lord Jesus Christ and thou shalt be saved"* (Acts 16:31).

But what does it mean to be "saved?" What is "salvation" and how does it work? What is a person saved *from*? Why is salvation needed?

And who is "the Lord Jesus Christ?" Why call Him "Lord?" What did Jesus do to make it possible for us to be saved?

Why is it necessary to "believe" on the Lord Jesus Christ? What does "believe" mean? Is faith the same thing as believing? What about my good works? Don't I need to do something more than just "believe" to be saved? Doesn't it matter how I live? Is it possible to lose my salvation after I have it? Could I become spiritually lost again?

Sometimes confusing words are used when talking about salvation. You may hear someone talk about "sanctification," or "justification," or "propitiation." What do all these big and formal words mean, and what do they have to do with being saved? We need clear, biblical answers in plain English.

This book is designed to provide the answers to these and many more questions. Instead of being a collection of various thoughts or opinions on what salvation means, this book is intended to express only one opinion: God's. It does not matter what any of us as mere humans think about salvation. Only God has the correct and complete answer. He has communicated that answer to us in His book, the Bible. Therefore, the chapters you are about to read are all based on what God has said in His Holy Word. It is our prayer that this book will be a help to you and glorifying to God.

Chapter 1

The Gospel

My friend, James Laomai, is from an outer island of Yap known as Fais. This is his story, a testimony, about how God worked in an unusual way in his life.

It was on a beautiful night that my older brother, Rolence, some of our cousins, and I went to go spear fishing off our island of Fais. I went out with them, but I went without fins, a flashlight, or a spear. That night as we were going along I would get the fish from one of the guys in our group. Then I would swim over to the floating cooler and put the fish in the cooler.

One time as I was swimming to the cooler I felt like I was stepping on something. I knew that it could not be the reef because we were far enough outside of the reef. Then, I felt something pulling on my leg. I still didn't know what was happening. Suddenly I was being pulled under the water by my leg. I started screaming and crying!

My brother, Rolence, swam over to me very fast and he speared the shark to get it to let go of me. He then took me to the beach where I could receive treatment. But the shark had taken a big bite out of my leg and they could not treat it on my island. So the plane had to come to take me to the main island of Yap. My brother saved my life that night.

Later, my brother heard the message about Jesus dying for our sins and he was saved. He started witnessing to me and talked to me about how Jesus could save and change my life too. On March 15, 2009, I asked Jesus to save me from my sin. My brother not only saved my life physically from the shark, he also told me how I could be saved spiritually by Jesus. My life has never been the same since! (Editor's note: James Laomai is affectionately called "Sharkey" by his friends and still bears the marks of that shark attack on his leg. James went on to graduate from Harvest Baptist Bible College, Guam, and is now serving as a pastor on the island of Ulithi).

Not everyone has such a dramatic story in their life. No one wants to be a shark snack! But we can all know the same spiritual salvation through the gospel of Jesus Christ. God works in the lives of people all over the world in millions of different settings and ways and circumstances. Even with all the different nations, islands, cultures, languages, backgrounds and experiences in the world, everyone comes to have a relationship with God in only *one* way – through faith in the Lord Jesus Christ. Jesus said of Himself, *"I am the way, the truth, and the life: no man comes unto the Father, but by me"* (John 14:6). This life-changing message about Jesus is known as "the gospel." There are lots of different religions in the world, but there is only one gospel message.

We cannot understand the whole topic of salvation without having a clear understanding of the gospel. The gospel is the message that tells us how to be saved. Getting the message right makes a heaven or hell difference! We must rightly understand and believe the gospel. We also must correctly, carefully and compassionately share the gospel with others.

> *There are lots of different religions in the world,*
> *but there is only one gospel message.*

GETTING THE GOSPEL RIGHT

What is the gospel? There is both a short answer and a long answer to that question. In a way, it is like trying to answer the question, "what is life about?" You could give a short answer to that question. But it is also true that you have to live life to keep understanding it. The lesson never ends. So it is with the gospel. There is a beginning point (and we can make a clear, definite statement about that), but there is no ending point. The gospel message keeps on impacting those who have received it. The gospel changes us not just at a point in time, but forever.

Because it makes an eternal difference, getting the message of the gospel right is of the highest importance. If a sick person goes to a doctor or hospital for help, they may receive a prescription for medicine to take. The directions for taking that medicine are extremely important. With some medications, if you do not take enough you will not get well. But if you take too much you might die! The message about how much medication to take and when to take it can potentially make a life or death difference. When it comes to the gospel, much more than mere physical, temporary life is at stake. The gospel makes a spiritual difference for eternity. We must be careful to get it right. There is only one place where we can get the true gospel message. It is from the Author of the message. It is from God, and God tells us in His Holy Word, the Bible, exactly what that saving message of the gospel is.

What IS the Gospel?

THE GOSPEL MESSAGE

The gospel is the grace of God in action.

The gospel is the love of God in its fullest display.

The gospel is the holiness of God demanded and satisfied.

The gospel is the purpose of God fulfilled

The gospel is the heart of God opened wide.

The gospel is the word of God worked out.

The gospel is the will of God obeyed.

The gospel is the only and eternal hope of man.

That man is mentioned last in this series is not by accident. While we tend to see the gospel as being about us, the truth is that the gospel is primarily about God and His gracious plan of salvation. He is the hero of the story. The gospel is God-centered, even though we in our day have made it more and more man-centered.

Through the gospel man is saved – gloriously and eternally saved. But that very salvation came not by the will of man nor by the work of man. It did not come with our help or by our hands. How could it? We have nothing to offer but our sin. The gospel is God's plan from beginning to end. The gospel is God's doing in every way. The gospel is the glory of God forever.

The central figure and the central focus of the gospel is the Lord Jesus Christ. In all of creation there is not to be found anything or anyone who could save sinful man from the righteous wrath of God. The answer had to come from outside of creation. But only God is outside of creation, for He created all things. So the answer must come from God and from God alone.

But God is God – He is eternal and cannot die. How can God pay for man's sin if God cannot die? The Second Person of the Trinity – the eternal Son of God – became man to die for mankind.[1] The God-Man, Jesus Christ, lived a sinless life and died a sacrificial death. The gospel is the amazing, majestic, powerful, glorious story of God's plan of redemption as displayed to the wicked, hell-deserving world when the Lord of glory was nailed to the cross for our sins. The gospel is the power of God unto salvation to all that believe (Romans 1:16).

---

1 See Chapters 3 and 4 to see how Jesus fulfilled this role.

The word "gospel" means "good news."[2] The gospel is such good news that it is in fact the *best* news one could ever hear. Other kinds of good news may make us happy for a time, but only the gospel's good news can make us both happy *and* holy for eternity.

The message of the gospel is summarized in the Bible in 1 Corinthians 15:1-4 (emphasis added).

*"Moreover, brethren, I declare unto you **the gospel** which I preached unto you, which also ye have received, and wherein ye stand; 2 By which also ye are saved, if ye keep in memory what I preached unto you, unless ye have believed in vain. 3 For I delivered unto you first of all that which I also received, how **that Christ died** for our sins according to the scriptures; 4 And **that he was buried,** and **that he rose again the third day** according to the scriptures."*

For clarification, some words have been highlighted. In these verses we see that *the gospel* is defined as having three essential[3] parts: 1) ***that Christ died*** – referring to the crucifixion of Jesus which paid for the penalty of our sin, 2) ***that he was buried*** –

---

2 The New Testament was written in Greek. The Greek word translated "gospel" is actually the word from which we get "evangel" and similar words, like "evangelist" and "evangelism." The first part of "evangel" is "ev" but used to be "eu," which is Greek for "good." The second part of the word is "angel" – yes, just like the spiritual being "angel," which means "messenger" or "message." Put together, ev angel = "good message" (or good news).

3 The word "essential" means that something must be included – it is necessary.

showing that Jesus truly died and had not simply passed out, and 3) ***that he rose again the third day*** – proving that Jesus had power even over death. So, the summary of the gospel is the death, burial and resurrection of Jesus Christ. This is not the *full* statement of the gospel, but it does include the most basic and necessary ingredients. As we shall see, believing the gospel means more than just believing the "facts" about the gospel. We are to have faith *in Jesus Christ Himself* and not just facts concerning Him.

> *The summary of the gospel is the death,*
> *burial and resurrection of Jesus Christ*

I love cake, especially chocolate cake. If I ask my wife how she makes the cake, or what the necessary ingredients are to make a cake, she will list several things for me: flour, baking soda, salt, oil, etc. All these items, and others, go into making a cake. But what if you just ate one of those ingredients? Eat some flour by itself – it tastes nothing like a cake! Swallow some oil or a tablespoon of salt. It is awful! You have to have all the ingredients together and then they have to be under intense heat for a while before you get the desired result.

The gospel is similar. We cannot just take one or two parts out of it. The gospel doesn't work that way. Salvation doesn't work that way. We can think of 1 Corinthians 15:1-4 as our "list of ingredients" for the gospel. Everything on the list is needed, exactly as it is given. As with making a cake, however, we soon realize that having the right list of ingredients is not enough. We also need to put those ingredients together in the right way and take them through the right process to end with the right result. The rest of this book examines the "ingredients" and how they are put together. For now, we will simply develop the basics of the gospel a little bit more.

As we saw in the passage above, *"Christ died for our sins."* The gospel is the good news we need because there is such bad news. The bad news is about "our sins." Every person who has ever lived, except Jesus, has sinned against God and against others. There are no exceptions. All of us have sinned and are sinners.[4] Because God is holy and righteous, He must punish sin. The punishment, or the "payment," for our sins must be holy and eternal, because we have sinned against God who is holy and eternal. None of us are holy, and none of us are eternal! So Jesus, the eternal Son of God, who was and is completely holy, died on the cross to offer Himself as the payment for our sins. When Jesus rose from the dead on the third day after the crucifixion, His resurrection proved that God the Father had fully accepted Christ's payment for our sins.

---
4 Romans 3:9-11, 3:23; 1 John 1:8-10.

Christ died for our sins – that is <u>very</u> good news!

If you or I had to pay for our own sins, that payment would have to last for eternity. That is why hell is an eternal place of torment. That is bad news! In fact, it is the worst possible news. But the good news, the "gospel," is the *best* possible news because *"Christ died for our sins."*

THE GOSPEL IN A VERSE

Romans 6:23 contains the heart of the gospel message in one verse. It tells us both the bad news and the good news. It also tells us something about how we receive this good news. *"For the wages of sin is death; but the gift of God is eternal life through Jesus Christ our Lord."*

The bad news:	The wages	of sin	is death
The good news:	The gift	of God	is eternal life

Through Jesus Christ our Lord

Notice the contrasts[5] – the opposites – in this verse:

1) The wages are contrasted with the gift When we talk about wages we mean "what we earn" or what we deserve. For exam-

---

5 A "contrast" is most often introduced by the word "but." When two things are the opposite of each other, they are contrasted. For example, light is the opposite of dark. Light and dark are contrasts.

ple, if you work for someone and they pay you for that work, you have "earned" that payment. Your wages are what you deserve for what you did. So the "wages of sin" means what you (and I) deserve for sinning. The first line ends with a description of what "sin" earns for us: death!

2) The contrast is the gift of God. A gift is the opposite of wages. Someone gives you a gift because they care about you, not because you worked for it. The gift is not earned by you; it is *given* to you. The gospel message is that we don't get what we deserve (death), but instead we are given what we *don't* deserve (eternal life).

3) There is also a strong contrast between sin and God which we should not overlook. God is the opposite of sin because God is completely holy.[6] It is precisely because of His holiness that God must demand a holy and eternal payment for sin. It is also precisely because of His holiness that God could (and did!) provide the only possible payment for our sin.[7]

The final contrast is between death and eternal life.

4) Because "life" in this verse is defined as being "eternal," that is also how we should understand "death" in this verse. This is not merely about physical death (which everyone will experience, whether saved or unsaved), but about *spiritual* death, meaning a

[6] The word "holy" means to be separated from sin and to God. To be "holy" is to be without sin. Only God is holy.

[7] This important point is given in Romans 3:25-26, which will be discussed later in Chapter 9.

separation *from* God for eternity. Spiritual death is, therefore, the opposite of eternal life – being *with* God for eternity. Which direction is *your* life going in?

Spiritual Death ⟵⟶ Spiritual Life
Separated from God for Eternity ⟵⟶ *With God for Eternity*

5) The last part of Romans 6:23 tells us **how God provides "the gift" of eternal life** It is *"through* (or "in") *Jesus Christ our Lord."* If someone gives you a gift, you don't pay for it. But *someone* paid for it! Even if the gift was not something purchased, but rather something made for you, someone other than you *did* something to provide that gift. God's gift of eternal life is free to all who will receive it. But it cost God. Eternal life is a *free* gift to us because Jesus paid the price on the cross. The cost is more than we can imagine. The price God the Father paid was the nailing of His Son to the cross.

It was not just the physical pain of crucifixion that was the payment. God also poured on Jesus all our sin and therefore all God's wrath.[8] Jesus took it all and payed for it completely. When the payment was completely done, Jesus said these last words from the cross: *"it is finished"* (John 19:30). That statement means "the debt is fully paid." There is nothing else that needs to be

The debt is fully paid! Nothing else is needed.

---
8 Isaiah 53:3-12 is a detailed prophecy of the crucifixion.

paid or could be paid. This is one of the main reasons why for someone to say "you need to add good works" to what Jesus has done is blasphemy.[9] That would be like telling Jesus, "Your death was good, but it wasn't good enough to completely pay for my sin, so I need to add something to it." I don't think any of us would really want to say that.

Although it will be covered in more detail later in the chapters on "Salvation in Jesus Christ," we should note here that the gift is not simply *"through Jesus Christ."* It is important to consider the whole phrase. The gift of eternal life is *"through Jesus Christ **our Lord**."* In addition to believing in *what* Jesus did (death and resurrection) our commitment is also to *who* Jesus is (our Lord). Jesus is Lord because he is fully God. He is *"the Lord of glory"* (1 Corinthians 2:8; James 2:1) and He is *"Lord of all"* (Acts 10:36). Jesus has *"all power* (authority) *in heaven and earth"* (Matthew 28:18). When the Philippian jailer asked Paul, *"What must I do to be saved?"* the response was, *"Believe on the Lord Jesus Christ, and thou shalt be saved"* (Acts 16:30-31). Jesus is both the Savior of our souls for eternity and the Lord of our lives for eternity.

The gospel is *"the power of God unto salvation"* (Romans 1:16) for anyone and everyone who believes. The highest purpose of the gospel is more than just our salvation, as wonderful as that is. The highest purpose of the gospel is the glory of God.[10]

---

9 "Blasphemy" means saying or thinking anything about God which is unworthy of Him.

10 See Philippians 2:10; John 17; 1 Corinthians 10:31; 2 Corinthians 4:6.

In eternity to come, all the saved from every land and from all time will sing the praises of the One who saved us.[11]

> *"The highest purpose of the gospel is the glory of God."*

Jesus began His ministry with these words: *"The time is fulfilled, and the kingdom of God is at hand: repent ye, and believe the gospel"* (Mark 1:15). This is what every person is called to do: *"repent and believe the gospel."* The gospel message is that Jesus Christ the Lord died for our sins (as the payment for our sins), was buried and then rose from the dead three days later (assuring victory over sin and death). Repent and believe. Repent by agreeing with God that you have sinned against Him and ask for God's forgiveness. Repent by turning away from your sin and turning to God. Believe in who Jesus is (the Lord) and what He has done (paid for your sins).

If you have not already done this, right now is the best moment to do so. A simple prayer for salvation might be worded something like this: *"God, I confess that I have sinned against You and others. I repent of my sins and ask Your forgiveness. I believe that Your holy Son, the Lord Jesus Christ, died to pay for my sins. Thank You God for that great gift. Help me to live for You and follow You as my Lord."*

And God says *"whosoever shall call upon the name of the Lord shall be saved"* (Rom. 10:13).

11 Revelation 5:9-14.

STUDY QUESTIONS

1. Why is it so important to get the gospel message *right*?

2. "There is only one place to get the true gospel message." What is that place?

3. What are the three essential parts of the gospel message (from 1 Corinthians 15:1-4)?

4. Since the gospel is the "good news," what is the "bad news" about?

5. Explain the meaning of Romans 6:23

6. What is the *highest* purpose of the gospel?

Chapter 2

The NEED for Salvation

It is easy for us human beings to confuse our needs with our wants. Sometimes they are the same. A man who is drowning both needs and wants a boat or someone to save him. But often our needs and wants are quite different. A person may want a huge feast, but what he truly *needs* is only a simple meal. This does not mean it is evil to want a huge feast, but we should not confuse it with what we really *need*. A feast may not actually rise to the level of need. And there are still other times when what we think we want is actually the opposite of that which we truly need. For example, a sick child may not *want* to get a shot of medicine and yet still seriously *need* that exact injection. So we can see it is important to think clearly about those things in life that are true needs. This is most important when we talk about ultimate things: our final destiny for eternity, heaven and hell.

God says we have a need for salvation. Every person has that same need. This is true even if they do not yet sense the need or even if they do not *want* salvation. Why do we all need salvation? What is it about God and about us that makes salvation so necessary? How does God provide for that need? Those questions are the focus of this present chapter.

The need for salvation begins with a story, and the story begins in a perfect, beautiful garden called Eden (Genesis 2 and 3). Into this paradise of a garden God placed the first two people – Adam and Eve.

In the beginning, Adam and Eve had everything they needed. It was beautiful and perfect in every way. Not only did they have all they needed for physical life, but also for spiritual life. They had unbroken fellowship with God. He walked with them and talked with them in the garden. There was no sickness, no death, no tears and no problems because there was no sin. God told them they could eat freely of all the trees in the garden – except one. They were not allowed to eat of *"the tree of the knowledge of good and evil"* (Genesis 2:17).[12] Since Adam and Eve already had the knowledge of *good*, God was protecting them from the knowledge of *evil*!

An enemy came into this garden. His name is Satan.[13] He was the highest of the angels at one time. But his pride led him to

---

12 The Bible does not explain to us what kind of tree the "tree of knowledge of good and evil" was, nor does the Bible tell us what the "fruit" of the tree was like. Perhaps we should not think of the fruit itself as having some kind of power to change people, but rather the very act of taking the fruit and eating the fruit, because it had been forbidden by God, was an act of evil. Once they had done evil (sinned) by eating the fruit, their eyes were opened to sin. That one sin opened the door for every other sin (see Romans 5:12ff).

13 "Satan" means "adversary" or "enemy." Satan is the enemy of God and of man. He is also called by descriptions such as: liar, deceiver, evil one, accuser of the brethren, destroyer, Lucifer.

revolt against God because he wanted to take the place of God.[14] Satan appeared in the garden in the form of a serpent[15] and talked with the woman in order to deceive her. It seems strange to us for anyone to actually talk to a serpent! But we must remember that in those early days of creation, before the curse of sin changed everything, it was evidently not such a surprising thing. It is likely that Adam and Eve were able to talk with the animals. In any case, Eve does not seem to be at all surprised by the conversation.

> *God was protecting them from the knowledge of evil!*

Satan deceived and tricked Eve into questioning God's Word and God's goodness. It is the same kind of trick Satan and his demons try to use in our own lives today. Satan led Eve to doubt God's Word and then to disobey God's Word. So she took of the fruit of the tree of the knowledge of good and evil and ate it, even though God had said they would certainly die in the day they ate of it (Genesis 2:17). Eve also gave this forbidden fruit to her husband, Adam, and he ate it too. Both of them sinned against God.

God is always faithful to what He says. That includes the warnings God gives about sin. Because God had said that their disobedience in this matter of eating the forbidden fruit would result in

---

14 You can read about the fall of Satan from heaven in the following passages: Isaiah 14:12-15; Ezekiel 28:11-19; Revelation 12:7-12.

15 A serpent is what we more commonly call a "snake."

death, He of course kept His word. Although it is jumping way into the future of the story, it is important for us to remember that God, who knows all things, knew that this penalty of death would one day lead to the sacrificial death of the Son, Jesus Christ, on the cross to pay for our sin. Yet God was still true to His word.

When God warned that man would die as a result of eating the forbidden fruit, He was speaking about both physical death and spiritual death. Something which is common with both kinds of death is the idea of separation. In physical death the spirit leaves (is separated from) the body. As God tells us through James "the body without the spirit is dead" (James 2:26). For a believer, "to be absent from the body is to be present with the Lord" (2 Corinthians 5:8). When the spirit of a person is separated from the body of the person, the result is physical death. Adam and Eve had been created by God to live continually. But after their sin they were forced to leave the garden and were no longer able to eat of the tree of life.[16] Adam and Eve began the slow process of physically dying.[17] In addition, as part of the curse, their time "living" was no longer without trouble. From then on their lives would include pain and suffering and trials and the hard things of life we have come to

---
16 Genesis 3:24. This is actually a display of the grace of God. If man had been able to continually live he would also continue to be in a state of sin and separation from God. It is interesting and comforting to note that in heaven God will once again provide the tree of life (Rev. 22:2; 14).

17 As a testimony of their perfection at creation, we are told Adam lived 930 years! See Genesis 5:5.

know. Even the ground (earth) was cursed (see Genesis 3:14-19).

Far worse than physical death is spiritual death. Remember that "death" involves a separation. The kind of separation that occurs because of spiritual death is separation from God. For the first time in their lives Adam and Eve no longer walked in fellowship with God. They could not be close to God because their sin had made a wall of separation between them and God. All of the rest of the story of salvation throughout the Bible is really about how God would Himself make a way for man to once again be in His presence – to no longer be separated from Him. As the New Testament explains, to have everlasting life means to eternally be with God, but everlasting death means to be eternally separated from God. Spiritual death is separation from God.[18] Spiritual life means nothing can separate us from God (Romans 8:35-39; John 10:27-30).

Even in judgment God provides a way for salvation

The disobedience in the Garden of Eden is a sad story. It is tragic and it ends with the curse of God upon Satan, man, woman and the earth. But there is one bright spot, one ray of hope which shines through even in this darkness. Even in judgment God provides a

---

[18] See for example John 3:36, 6:40 & 47; Romans 6:23; 2 Thessalonians 2:11-12.

way for salvation. As God was proclaiming His judgment upon the serpent He included this promise: *"And I will put enmity between thee and the woman, and between thy seed and her seed; it shall bruise thy head, and thou shalt bruise his heel"* (Gen 3:15). We might call this the "first gospel" because it provides hope of a future Deliverer.[19] From the seed of the woman would come someone who will wage war with Satan. Although the Deliverer's "heel" will be bruised (He will suffer pain) by Satan and his followers, Satan will have his head bruised (literally *"crushed"*), resulting in his total defeat. The gospel in this passage, like its fulfillment, is only in "seed" form. We only see here the potential and not the fruit of the gospel. Nevertheless, there is hope. A Deliverer, a Savior, will come.

There is much more to this story. You and I are part of the story. For one thing, every person who has ever been born came from that first couple – Adam and Eve. We all inherited from them something dark and terrible and spiritually fatal. Through Adam each one of us has inherited a sin nature. This sin nature has been part of who we are since the time of our conception, just like our DNA.[20]

---

19 A "deliverer" is someone who "delivers" or "saves" us from our enemy. In this case, the enemy is Satan and our own sin. The One who delivers or saves us is Jesus Christ. Jesus, the Son of God, is the One the Father sent to pay the penalty for our sins and defeat Satan. Through faith in Jesus we are saved (delivered).

20 DNA refers to the chemical makeup of our genes. Our genetic makeup determines what we are like, male or female, short or tall, eye color, hair color, etc. The reason we look similar as human beings is because we share the same basic genetic makeup. The reason there are differences between us is that there are slight differences in our genes. The point we are making in this

David confesses in Psalm 51:5 *"Behold, I was brought forth in iniquity, and in sin my mother conceived me"* (see also Psalm 58:3, John 3:6). From the moment of conception we have had a sin nature.

Romans 5:12-21 speaks about this inherited sin nature in much more detail. For now, we will just consider what the Apostle Paul wrote in Romans 5:12: *"Wherefore, as by one man sin entered into the world, and death by sin; and so death passed upon all men, for that all have sinned."* The "one man" by whom "sin entered into the world" is Adam. God is telling us here that the sin nature is passed down specifically by the man. We also see the result *"and death by sin; and so death passed upon all men."* The penalty for sin, as it was for Adam and Eve in the garden, is death. Again, this is not only talking about physical death (we will all die physically), but also about spiritual death (we are all "separated from God" and therefore spiritually dead) until something is done about the sin problem.

In addition, we also see from Romans 5:12 that *"all have sinned"* (see also Romans 3:10-11, 23). Our problem is not simply that Adam sinned and that we inherited his sin nature. It is worse than that because all of us have actively sinned by choosing to sin. In other words, we have a sin nature *and* we have personally sinned. We were born with a sin nature and we have followed that sin

---

chapter is that in the same way we are born with a certain DNA (genes) which we do not choose (we are who we are naturally), we also all are born with a sin nature.

nature. You might say that sin is a natural part of who we are. We are not basically good. We are basically sinners.

In Romans 7 Paul states the problem this way: *"For I know that in me (that is, in my flesh,) dwells no good thing: for to will is present with me; but how to perform that which is good I find not"* (Romans 7:18). God does not look at us and think that we are part good and part bad. That is the way *we* often think of ourselves. But God, the perfect, holy Judge sees us exactly as we are. When we agree with God we say with Paul *"in me, in my flesh, **nothing** good dwells."* Isaiah is even more bold: *"But we are all as an unclean thing, and all our righteousnesses are as filthy rags; and we all do fade as a leaf; and our iniquities, like the wind, have taken us away"* (Isaiah 64:6). Even the "righteous" things we think we do are like "filthy rags" to God because of our sin nature. For example, we may do some kind thing for someone, but in our heart our motive is wrong. Some of the things we do may indeed be better than other things we do, but *none* of them count toward our righteousness in God's eyes. This does not mean that everyone is guilty of the same amount or kind of sin, but rather that everyone is guilty of sin in at least some measure. There is no one who is without sin and we are all guilty before God. Something must be done about the sin problem!

> *We are not basically good.*
> *We are basically sinners!*

Consider what Paul wrote in Ephesians 2:1-3:

And you hath he quickened, who were **dead** *in trespasses and sins; ² Wherein in time past ye walked according to the course of this world, according to the prince of the power of the air, the spirit that now works in the children of disobedience: ³ Among whom also we* **all** *had our conversation (way of living) in times past in the lusts of our flesh, fulfilling the desires of the flesh and of the mind; and were* **by nature the children of wrath**, *even as others* (emphasis added).

We all have a need for salvation because we are all lost – we have all sinned. This is what makes the good news of the Gospel so important. It is such "good" news because the truth about our sin is such "bad" news. We cannot get to heaven while we still have the guilt of sin. Holy God cannot and will not allow *any* sin into His presence. *"Thou art of purer eyes than to behold evil, and canst not look on iniquity"* (Habakkuk 1:13). We do not come to the King on our own terms; we come to Him only on His terms. The King says the entrance requirement to heaven is that we must be *perfect* (Matthew 5:48; Galatians 3:10; 1 Peter 1:15; James 2:10). No one who ever lived, except for Jesus Christ, is perfect. No one is without sin (Romans 3:23). Therefore, everyone has the same need of salvation.

> *The King says the entrance requirement to heaven is that we must be perfect*

Once we understand that we are sinners and that we must one day come before God, who, because He is holy and just *must* punish sin and not allow sinners into His presence, then we also understand our need for a Savior. Some people might avoid going to a doctor because they know that the news they will receive will not be good. However, not taking a trip to the doctor will not change the health problem they have! It might give a temporary peace of mind because they cannot see the great danger ahead of them. But it doesn't take away the danger; it just ignores it. This is the same for people who do not take time to read God's Word or listen to what God says about their sin and their need of salvation. Their situation does not get better by not thinking about it. Their situation just gets worse![21] We all need to come to the Great Physician, God, so that He can both show us our need and show us His salvation.

The good news is that God *has* provided a way for us to be saved. He has paid the price. He has purchased our salvation by the death of Christ on the cross! This chapter is only designed to make the case that we *all* need salvation. For the answer to that eternal need, please read carefully the chapters on *The Gospel* (chapter 1), *Salvation in Jesus Christ* (chapters 3 & 4), and *Receiving Salvation* (chapter 5). God's great and gracious plan from the beginning has been to provide the way for people to have their sins

---

[21] This illustration was provided by Bryan Lenartz.

forgiven and to be able to live with Him in the glory of Heaven for eternity. Our first step is to see, and agree, that we are sinners and that we have a desperate need for salvation.

STUDY QUESTIONS FOR CHAPTER 2

1. When God commanded Adam and Eve to not eat of the tree of the knowledge of good and evil, what was God protecting them from?

2. Read Genesis 3:1-6. In your own words, tell how Satan tricked (deceived) Eve to disobey God.

3. Does Satan use the same tactics to deceive people today? How?

4. To have everlasting (eternal) life means to be eternally with God. What does eternal death mean?

5. According to the Bible, are people basically good or basically bad? Why do you say that?

6. What is the entrance requirement into heaven?

7. How does Genesis 3:15 give the promise of what we might call "the first gospel"?

Chapter 3

Salvation in Jesus Christ

Part 1: WHO JESUS IS

If you ask a man to do something for you, he has to be in a position to do what you ask, he has to be able to do it, and he must be willing to do it. For example, if you ask someone to fly you to a place far away, that person has to be a pilot, have a plane available, be able to fly that plane and be willing to take you. In other words, the person has to be qualified, willing and able.

When it comes to our salvation, whoever and whatever we are trusting to save us must be qualified to save us, willing to save us and able to save us. In all the universe there is only one Person who is qualified, willing and able to save us: Jesus Christ. What is it that makes Jesus qualified? How do we know He is willing? How can we be sure He is able? These next two chapters will seek to answer those questions. We will do so by looking especially at who Jesus is (this chapter) and what Jesus did (next chapter). We will see that Jesus, and only Jesus, is qualified, willing and able to take us to a special far-away place called Heaven. *Only Jesus can save us from our sin and give us eternal life.*

What would you answer if Jesus asked you this question: "Who do you say that I am?"

Jesus asked His disciples, *"Who do you say that I am?"* (Matthew 16:15). Of all the questions that they (or you or I) need to answer, this question is the most important! If we do not know who Jesus is we cannot understand what Jesus did. And if we do not understand and put our trust in what Jesus did for us, we cannot be saved. Or, to put it in a more positive way, once we come to understand who Jesus is we can more easily see how He could save us. What would you answer if Jesus asked *you* this question: *"Who do you say that I am?"*

We need Jesus to open our eyes to see who He really is!

JESUS IS FULLY GOD

God is a Trinity. "Trinity" means "three-in-one." God is made up of Three Persons (Father, Son and Holy Spirit). But these Three Persons are a unity, or "united" in One God. Three Persons in One God. All Three Persons are exactly equal in all ways.[22] For example, each Person has the same power, the same attributes, the same character, and so on. In this chapter we are focusing on the Second Person of the Godhead – the Son of God, Jesus Christ. Our purpose here is to show how the Bible proves that Jesus Christ is fully God.

---

22 Their roles (or functions) within the Trinity are different, but they all have the same attributes and character.

*Because Jesus is fully God
He is able to fully save.*

1. *The title "God" is used of Jesus*

Jesus is called *"our God and Savior"* (2 Peter 2:1) and *"the great God and Savior"* (Titus 2:13). When the Apostle Thomas saw Jesus alive after the resurrection, he called out, *"My Lord and my God."* Paul wrote to the church at Rome about Christ and described Him as the one *"who is over all, God blessed forever. Amen"* (Romans 9:5). At the beginning of the Gospel of John we read, *"In the beginning was the Word, and the Word was with God, and the Word was God"* (John 1:1). Again and again we see that Jesus is more than "like" God; Jesus *is* God. Because Jesus is fully God He is able to fully save.

2. *The title "Lord" is used of Jesus*

Jesus is referred to as *"the Lord Jesus Christ"* 84 times in the New Testament. Another 35 times He is called simply *"the Lord Jesus."* Saying that Jesus is "the Lord" means that He is the Master over all and that He rules over all. This is a title that can only be used of God,[23] so this means that Jesus is clearly presented to us in Scrip-

23 The word "lord" can also simply mean "master" or a title of respect like "sir" without any reference to God. However, it is used in a special way in the New Testament to speak of Jesus. He is called "the Lord" and not simply "a lord." Also, many of the references to Jesus as Lord are connected back to Old Testament passages that are clearly talking about God (for instance, compare Matthew 3:3 with Isaiah 40:3, or Psalm 110:1 with Matthew 22:44). Jesus is "the Lord of glory" (1 Corinthians 2:8).

ture as God. One day everyone who has ever lived will agree that Jesus is Lord. Philippians 2:9-11 says,

"Wherefore God also hath highly exalted him, and given him a name which is above every name: [10] That at the name of Jesus every knee should bow, of things in heaven, and things in earth, and things under the earth; [11] And that every tongue should confess that Jesus Christ is Lord, to the glory of God the Father."

When Jesus returns to rule over all the earth as the conquering King it will be as *"the KING OF KINGS AND LORD OF LORDS"* (Revelation 19:16).

3. *Other indications that Jesus is God*

In addition to noting that Jesus is clearly called both "God" and "Lord" a number of times in the Bible there are other indications of His Deity.[24] Jesus is spoken of as being eternal[25] and as being the Creator of all things.[26] Since only God is eternal and since only God is the Creator of all, Jesus must be God. Jesus is referred to as "Christ" (which means "Messiah") and is therefore the fulfillment

---

24 "Deity" is a theological word referring to that which is "God" and which has divine character or attributes.
25 See Micah 5:2; Isaiah 9:6; John 1:1; John 8:58; John 17:5.
26 John 1:1-3; Colossians 1:16-17; Hebrews 1:2; Hebrews 1:10-12.

of all the Old Testament prophecies concerning Messiah. Jesus is "the Son of God" (not simply a son of God). When Jesus called Himself "God's Son," the Jewish leaders took up stones to stone Him. Why would they do that? Because they thought it was blasphemy since that meant He was saying He was *equal* with God (see John 5:15-23).

Jesus said *"I and the Father are One"* (John 10:30) and *"He that has seen Me has seen the Father"* (John 14:9), meaning that Jesus fully and accurately reveals what God the Father is like because Jesus is also fully God (see also Colossians 1:19 and 2:9). In fact, Jesus fully shared the glory of God the Father before the world was created (John 17:5) because Jesus is God.

By His astonishing miracles, Jesus demonstrated that He is God. He caused the blind to see and the deaf to hear. He healed the lame so that they could walk. He cast out demons. He stilled storms with a word. He fed over 5,000 at one time. He raised the dead back to life. Greatest of all, He Himself rose from the dead, proving His victory over sin and death and proving that He is God (Romans 1:4).

Think of this wonderful truth – that Holy God Himself came to earth to save sinful man! This is the most precious jewel of all religious thought. God the Son died for our sins. Jesus came to earth for that very purpose (John 12:27).

Not only is Jesus fully God, He is also fully man. He is 100%

God and He is also 100% human. We have considered some passages from the Bible which demonstrate that Jesus is God. It is just as important that we also understand the full humanity of Jesus.

JESUS IS FULLY MAN

As we have seen, Jesus died for our sin. But God is eternal and He can never die. And Jesus is fully God. So *how* could Jesus ever die for our sin? The amazing answer to that question is that God became man and He did so without ceasing to be God. God the Son was born as a human baby in the village of Bethlehem over 2,000 years ago.

1. *The Virgin Birth*

When we think of the full humanity of Jesus Christ we must begin with the virgin birth. The Bible describes the miracle of the virgin birth this way:

Now the birth of Jesus Christ was on this wise: When as his mother Mary was espoused to Joseph, before they came together, she was found with child of the Holy Ghost. [19] *Then Joseph her husband, being a just man, and not willing to make her a public example, was minded to put her away privately.* [20] *But while he thought on these things, behold, the angel of the Lord appeared unto him in a dream, saying, Joseph, thou son of David, fear not to take unto thee Mary thy wife: for that which is conceived in her is of the Holy Ghost. [21] And she shall bring forth a son, and thou shalt call his name JESUS: for he shall save his people from their sins. [22] Now all this was done, that it might be fulfilled which was spoken of the Lord by the prophet, saying, [23] Behold, a virgin shall be with child, and shall bring forth a son, and they shall call his name Emmanuel, which being interpreted is, God with us. [24] Then Joseph being raised from sleep did as the angel of the Lord had bidden him, and took unto him his wife: [25] And knew her not till she had brought forth her firstborn son: and he called his name JESUS (Matthew 1:18-25).*

As we can see from this account, the human mother of Jesus was Mary, but there was no human father. Instead, Jesus was born of the Holy Spirit. We are never told exactly how that happened and we do not need to know the details (or else we would have been told). The most and the least we can say is that it was a miraculous event. The text also tells us that Mary did not "know" her husband Joseph until after the birth of Jesus. Thus, the account is not simply the "virgin conception," but the "virgin birth." Why is the virgin birth so important? Consider this:

A. God's promise from the beginning was that He would bring forth from the *"seed of the woman"* (Genesis 3:15) a Deliverer. As Paul explains in Galatians 4:4-5, *"But when the fullness of the time was come, God sent forth his Son, made of a woman, made under the law, ⁵ To redeem them that were under the law, that we might receive the adoption of sons."* The answer to man's sin problem was not provided by mankind; it was provided by God. This is a reminder that we cannot save ourselves. Salvation must be of the Lord. God the Father sent His Son, Jesus Christ, to die for our sins and to provide the gift of eternal life to all who believe.

> *The gift of eternal life given by the*
> *Father to all who believe in the Son*

B. The virgin birth made it possible for Jesus to be both fully God (born of the Holy Spirit) and fully man (born of Mary). If Jesus had been only fully God or only fully man He could not have saved us from our sin. By means of the virgin birth, Jesus is both God and man. This is beyond our full understanding, but the Bible consistently presents Jesus as being fully God without losing any of what it means to be man and Jesus is fully man without losing any of what it means to be God. He is both God and man. He is not half God and half man, but 100% God and 100% man. The only way for this to happen is by the virgin birth.

C. Because inherited sin is passed down through the first human father (Adam)[27] it is significant to note that Jesus had no human father. Because the "father" was the Holy Spirit, the child born of Mary was said to be "holy" as well (Luke 1:35). Jesus had to be a perfect and sinless sacrifice in order to pay for our sins. This was true of Him even from conception.[28]

2. Jesus Had a Human Body & Human Limitations

Jesus, as God, has existed forever. But He came to earth over 2,000 years ago, born as a real human baby in Bethlehem, Israel. His human life began at conception. He grew as a child *"And Jesus increased in wisdom and stature, and in favor with God and man"* (Luke 2:52). When the people of Jesus' day saw Him they did not think of Him as God but as a mere man.[29] They could not imagine that He was *also* God.[30] But they had no doubt He was fully human. Jesus had a real physical body just like we do. He knew what it was to hunger and thirst. He experienced being tired. He needed sleep. He expressed emotions like joy and anger and sadness. Jesus also experienced pain. When Jesus was nailed to the

27 See Romans 5:12-21.
28 Of course, God the Son has always been perfectly holy. What needed to be shown was that Jesus as the Son of Man (in His humanity) was without sin (and therefore holy) even from the time He was conceived.
29 See Matthew 13:53-58.
30 This is something they would have to learn and believe about Him. Even Jesus' own younger brothers, who grew up with Him and knew Him very well, did not believe Jesus was anything other than a mere man (John 7:5) until after His resurrection (Acts 1:14).

cross and suffered there for hours, He felt real pain, more than we can ever imagine. In fact, this is one of the important reasons[31] for Jesus having a physical body – that He would be able to *suffer* the pain of death to pay for our sins (Hebrews 2:9; 1 Peter 3:18).

The prophet Isaiah gave this amazing prophecy about the Messiah who would one day come to earth: *"For unto us **a child** is born, unto us **a son** is given: and the government shall be upon his shoulder: and his name shall be called Wonderful, Counsellor, **The mighty God**, The **everlasting Father**, The Prince of Peace"* (Isaiah 9:6, emphasis added). Isaiah said that Christ[32] would be both man (born as a child, a son) and God (mighty God, everlasting Father). This of course would take a miracle, and that is exactly what God provided: a miracle beyond our understanding.

Jesus, the Son of God, came "in the flesh" which is what the word "incarnation" means.[33] John 1:1 says of Jesus (who is here called "the Word"), *"In the beginning was the Word, and the Word was with God, and the Word was God."* Notice especially how this verse ends, *"and the Word was God,"* which reminds us of the full Deity of Jesus.[34]

Later in the same chapter we read, *"And the Word was made flesh,*

---

31 We will discuss other reasons in the next chapter of this book.
32 "Christ" is the Greek word for "Messiah" or "Anointed One."
33 "Incarnation" literally mean "in flesh" and this reminds us that Jesus had a real flesh and bone human body.
34 We must beware of false religions, like Jehovah's Witnesses, who change John 1:1 because they do not believe that Jesus is God. There can be no salvation if Jesus is not God because it took a perfect, holy, eternal sacrifice to save us. In many places the Bible clearly declares the Deity of Jesus – He is God.

and dwelt among us, (and we beheld his glory, the glory as of the only begotten of the Father,) full of grace and truth" (John 1:14). It is this being *"made flesh"* which points to the humanity of Jesus. He had a real human body. His body could hunger and thirst and grow tired. And His body could be nailed to a cross.

3. The Kenosis of Jesus

The word "kenosis" comes from a Greek word found in Philippians 2:7, and it means to "empty" oneself of something. When Jesus came from heaven to earth He "emptied" Himself of His rightful status and privilege as God.[35] That is, Jesus *knew* that even though He has always deserved to be worshipped as God, by coming to earth as a man He would be rejected instead of worshipped. He was willing to "empty" or "put aside" that right in order to humble Himself and come as a man to earth. Here is the full passage in Philippians 2:5-11:

"Let this mind be in you, which was also in Christ Jesus: ⁶ Who, being in the form of God, thought it not robbery to be equal with God: ⁷ But made himself of no reputation, and took upon him the form of a servant, and was made in the likeness of men: ⁸ And being found in fashion as a man, he humbled himself, and became obedient unto death, even the

---

35 Jesus, of course, never ceased being God. He has always been and always will be fully God.

death of the cross. ⁹ Wherefore God also hath highly exalted him, and given him a name which is above every name: ¹⁰ That at the name of Jesus every knee should bow, of things in heaven, and things in earth, and things under the earth; ¹¹ And that every tongue should confess that Jesus Christ is Lord, to the glory of God the Father."

Here are several observations from this passage:

1. "*Being in the form of God*" means being exactly like God (Hebrews 11:3)

2. "*thought it not robbery to be equal with God*" means that even though Jesus was fully "equal with God" He did not "grasp" or cling to that privilege.[36] He never ceased to be fully God, but He was willing to let go of the privilege of being treated as God.

3. "*But made himself of no reputation*" Means Jesus emptied Himself of the right to be seen as God and worshipped as God. Remember that Jesus has *always* deserved to be worshipped as God, even while here on earth, but He humbly laid aside that privilege.

4. "*and took upon himself the form of a servant*" reminds us that Jesus did not come to earth like a king but as a servant. A servant

---

[36] The word "robbery" in this verse means to "take hold of" or "hold onto" something. Here the meaning is not about robbery (stealing) but "holding onto" His status of being equal with God. This means Jesus was willing to let it go instead of holding onto it.

owns nothing and has no rights. This is a further description of the humility of Jesus.

5. "*and was made in the likeness of men*" means that Jesus actually and fully became a man. Everyone who saw Jesus saw Him as a real man. There was no doubt in their minds that Jesus was fully human.

6. "*and being found in fashion as a man, he humbled himself, and became obedient unto death, even the death of the cross*" means that Jesus "humbled *himself*" (it was not something forced upon Him, but rather something He chose). This verse also tells us of the full obedience of Jesus to the Father's will for Him, even though it meant *"the death of the cross."*

7. *Verses 9-11* explain that since Jesus was willing to do this (verses 5-8) He has been *"highly exalted"* and given a name above all names. He will be forever praised by every person who has ever lived, and all of this will bring glory to the Father.

Summary

As was pointed out at the beginning of this chapter, for someone to be able to save us from the guilt and penalty of our sins that person would have to be in a *position* of authority to save us, be *willing* to save us, and be *able* to save us. In all the universe and in all time there is only One who meets all of those requirements. Jesus is the only One who can save. *"Neither is there salvation in any other: for there is none other name under heaven given among men, whereby we must be saved"* (Acts 4:12). Jesus very clearly stated: *"I am the way, the truth, and the life: no man cometh unto the Father, but by me"* (John 14:6). Jesus is in a position to save us because He is Holy God and Perfect Man. Jesus is willing to save us. *"I am come that they might have life, and that they might have it more abundantly. ¹¹ I am the good shepherd: the good shepherd giveth his life for the sheep"* (John 10:10-11). And because Jesus died on the cross as the sinless sacrifice for our sins, Jesus is able to save us. Peter wrote that we are saved *"...with the precious blood of Christ, as of a lamb without blemish and without spot"* (1 Peter 1:19). We agree with the Apostle Paul when he said, *"Thanks be unto God for his unspeakable gift!"* (2 Corinthians 9:15).[37]

The Savior had to be fully God and a fully man at the same time. He had to be completely divine and completely human. If He had been only God, He could not have died (for it is impossible for God, Who is eternal, to die). If He had been only man, He would not have been perfectly without sin (for every human being is a sinner by birth and by choice). But Jesus is God who came in the flesh.[38] He was able to not sin and He was able to die for our sin. Jesus is the only perfect sacrifice for our sin. Because of His great love He was willing to save us. We will join our voices

[37] The gift of God in giving Jesus Christ (John 3:16; John 4:10) is here said by Paul to be "unspeakable." The Greek word translated "unspeakable" refers to something which is so great that it is beyond our ability to describe it.
[38] John 1:1-3 and John 1:14.

in praise to Him for all eternity!

"Worthy is the Lamb that was slain to receive power, and riches, and wisdom, and strength, and honor, and glory, and blessing. [13] And every creature which is in heaven, and on the earth, and under the earth, and such as are in the sea, and all that are in them, heard I saying, Blessing, and honor, and glory, and power, be unto him that sits upon the throne, and unto the Lamb for ever and ever"
(Revelation 5:12-13).

STUDY QUESTIONS FOR CHAPTER 3

1. What would you answer if Jesus asked *you* this question: "Who do you say that I am?"

2. Give at least three ways the Bible shows that Jesus is fully God.

3. How do we know that the physical body Jesus had was a real body?

4. What did Jesus "empty" Himself of when He came to earth (Phil. 2:7)?

5. Why did Jesus have to be *both* fully God *and* fully human to save us?

6. Read Philippians 2:9-11. What do these verses tell us about Jesus?

Chapter 4

Salvation in Jesus Christ

Part 2: WHAT JESUS DID

We saw in the last chapter that *who* Jesus is makes Him qualified, willing and able to be our Savior. But what did He have to *do* to actually save us? We can narrow our answer down to two specific points: 1) Jesus had to live a perfect sinless life for us, and 2) Jesus had to die a perfect sacrificial death for us.[39]

A PERFECT SINLESS LIFE

Jesus is the only person who has ever lived who never sinned. Every one of us has broken God's righteous law and failed to bring Him glory. The way the Bible says it is like this: *"For all have sinned, and come short of the glory of God"* (Romans 3:23).

Jesus did something we could never do – He perfectly obeyed the law of God and He perfectly glorified the Father (John 17:4).

Jesus was sinless because He perfectly obeyed the law of God. Scripture repeatedly declares the sinlessness of our Savior. The Apostle John wrote, *"And ye know that he was manifested[40] to take*

---

39 We could also technically add the necessity of the resurrection here, since it is part of the Gospel message (see chapter 1), but we will include it in the section on Jesus' death since it proves His victory over death.

40 "Manifested" means to "make known" or to "make visible."

away our sins; and in him is no sin" (1 John 3:5). Paul said of Jesus that *"He knew no sin"* (2 Corinthians 5:21). Peter confirms this by saying of Jesus, *"Who did no sin, neither was guile found in his mouth"* (1 Peter 2:22). We are saved by the sinless sacrifice of Jesus, *"with the precious blood of Christ, as of a lamb without blemish and without spot"* (1 Peter 1:19). Even when Satan himself tempted Jesus three times in the wilderness (see Matthew 4:1-10) Jesus answered each temptation with Scripture and obedience.[41] In the book of Hebrews we find several key statements about the obedience of Jesus when He was tempted. *"For in that He Himself has suffered, being tempted, He is able to aid those who are tempted"* (Hebrews 2:18). *"For we have not an high priest which cannot be touched with the feeling of our infirmities; but was in all points tempted like as we are, yet without sin. ¹⁶ Let us therefore come boldly unto the throne of grace, that we may obtain mercy, and find grace to help in time of need"* (Hebrews 4:15-16).

Jesus said of His obedience to the Father's will, *"I always do those things that please Him"* (John 8:29), and He prayed to the Father on the night before His death, *"I have glorified thee on the earth: I have finished the work which thou gavest me to do"* (John 17:4). Jesus was perfectly obedient to the Father's will, even to the point of death. Philippians 2:8 says, *"He humbled himself, and became obedient unto*

---

41 Jesus was likely tempted much more than the three times we are told about. Luke 4:2, for instance, says that Jesus was tempted 40 days by the devil. And Luke 4:13 says that the devil "departed from him for a season" which indicates the devil likely returned again and again.

death, even the death of the cross."

The night before Jesus was crucified He prayed in the garden of Gethsemane saying, *"Father, if thou be willing, remove this cup from me: nevertheless, not my will, but thine, be done"* (Luke 22:42). In all His life, and even to the point of death, Jesus never sinned, but rather completely and joyfully (Hebrews 12:2) obeyed the Father's will, always bringing glory to the Father (John 17:4).

In the Old Testament, the lamb that was sacrificed for the sin of the people had to be without blemish.[42] This was a way of reminding the people that God is holy, and only a sacrifice which met His requirements could be accepted by Him. When John the Baptist saw Jesus coming John said, *"Behold! The Lamb of God who takes away the sin of the world!"* (John 1:29).

Jesus would one day be the perfect sacrifice. But first He had to live a righteous, sinless, perfect life. Because Jesus never sinned, He proved that He was qualified to be the perfect sacrifice for sin. Jesus had to live a holy life in order to be the holy sacrifice. As Peter would later write, our sins were paid for *"with the precious blood of Christ, as of a lamb without blemish and without spot"* (1 Peter 1:19).

The righteousness of Jesus did even more than make His sacrifice possible for us. By His complete obedience to the Law, by His perfect submission to the Father, and by His perfectly sinless

---

42 A "blemish" is any kind of flaw or defect. The lamb had to be without any problems. It had to look perfect. See Exodus 12:5, Leviticus 1:3, 10, and 3:1 for some examples of this requirement in the Old Testament.

life, Jesus also provided for us *righteousness*. By paying for our sin on the cross Jesus made it possible for our sin to be removed. But Jesus did more than that. Not only is something taken away, something is also given to us. Our sins are taken away, and in addition, His righteousness is given to us.

> *The debt is fully paid! Nothing else is needed.*

Imagine you held in your hand a bill or some kind of a debt you could never pay. If someone came and paid your full debt for you, that would be awesome. But your hands would then be empty. Now imagine if someone not only took away your debt, but *also* placed into your hands a huge fortune! That is like what Jesus did for us. His death on the cross paid for our debt of sin. But He gives us something more: He gives us His righteousness. When God the Father looks down on a believer, He sees the righteousness of Christ. Here is how Paul explained it to the Corinthians: *"For he* (God) *hath made him* (Jesus) *to be sin for us, who knew no sin; that we might be made the righteousness of God in him"* (2 Corinthians 5:21). Notice that this verse has two main parts. The first half of the verse talks about Jesus, *"who knew no sin,"* taking on our sin. The second half of the verse talks about what we receive, *"that we might be made the righteousness of God in him."* This is the "give and take" of the Gospel: Jesus took our sin and Jesus gives us His righteousness. The perfect obedience of Jesus provides righteousness for us. As Paul wrote to the Romans, *"So by the obedience of one shall many be made righteous"* (Romans 5:19).

A PERFECT SACRIFICIAL DEATH

Our salvation depends on the perfect sinless life of Jesus. However, if Jesus had *only* lived a perfectly sinless life we would still be in our sin. Something else was needed. Jesus also had to die a perfect sacrificial death. His perfection in life proved that He was qualified to die for our sins. A person may *qualify* for a job if they meet certain requirements, like having the right education or experience. Of all the people who have ever lived, only Jesus has qualified to be our Savior. He met God's requirements because He was holy (sinless) and eternal (since He is God). One more thing was needed: Jesus had to actually shed His blood on the cross for us. He had to die a perfect sacrificial death.

Imagine if someone took you to a store and offered to buy you something you could not afford. That person would be qualified to make the purchase for you if he or she had enough money. But you could not get that item in the store *unless* that person actually *paid* for it. It is not enough for the person to meet the requirements of being able to pay; he or she also had to actually pay. The same kind of thing is true with Jesus. He met the requirements of being able to pay for our sin, but He also had to actually make the payment. Jesus had to die for us.

> *We are saved "with the precious blood of Christ,
> as of a lamb without blemish and without spot"*

When we say Jesus' death had to be a *perfect sacrificial death* we mean first of all that He had to be perfect (sinless) so that we could be saved *"with the precious blood of Christ, as of a lamb without blemish and without spot"* (1 Peter 1:19). Secondly, we mean His death had to be *sacrificial*. That is, He had to die *for* us. Since we spent the first part of this chapter focusing on the sinless perfection of Jesus, we will now turn our attention to the sacrificial nature of His death for us.

A *sacrifice* involves giving up something for the sake or benefit of someone else. For example, parents may sacrifice (give up) something they would like to have in order to provide something for their children. A man may sacrifice his time in order to help a friend. In war, a soldier may sacrifice his life in order to save other soldiers. In all these examples we see that a person who is making a sacrifice pays some kind of price (money, time, life). There is a cost for making a sacrifice. Sometimes that cost is very high. The most costly, precious sacrifice ever given was the death of Jesus on the cross. Because of God's great love (John 3:16; Romans 5:8) He sent His Son to be the sacrifice for our sins. God the Father sacrificed His Son. Romans 8:32 says, *"He that spared not his own Son, but delivered him up for us all, how shall he not with him also freely give us all things?"* Also, because Jesus willingly came to earth and went to the cross, the Bible says that Jesus sacrificed Himself (Hebrews 9:26; 10:12; John 10:17-18).

> *Jesus was our "substitutionary" sacrifice. We should have been nailed to that cross, but Jesus took our place; He was our substitute.*

The sacrifice of Jesus on the cross is also called a *substitutionary* sacrifice. The main idea is that of a *substitute*. If a teacher is not able to teach her class, another person may be asked to teach *in the place of* the absent teacher. We call this person a "substitute teacher." In many sports one player may play *in the place of* another player as a "substitute." As we can see, the meaning of *substitute* is that something is done *in the place of* someone else. Jesus died on the cross as our substitute; He died *in our place*. We deserve to die for our sins. We should have been nailed to that cross, but Jesus took our place; He was our substitute. We could never pay the full price for our sins. Since we are neither perfect nor eternal, our payment, our dying for sin, would go on forever. But Jesus as our substitute sacrificed Himself in our place. He died for us. *"But God commendeth* (showed or demonstrated) *his love toward us,* *in that, while we were yet sinners, **Christ died for us**"* (Romans 5:8). Jesus became our substitutionary sacrifice.

Because Jesus died for our sins, whoever believes in Him has everlasting life.[43] Later, in Chapter 9, we will also see how Jesus' substitutionary sacrifice brings about redemption and justification for us.

Sometimes theologians use the word "atonement" to talk about the sacrifice of Jesus for our sins. The word *atonement* refers to what Jesus did to reconcile[44] God and man. People who are not saved are enemies of God; they are at war with God and living in rebellion to God. There is nothing mankind could ever do to make peace with God and be reconciled to Him. So God made a way of having peace with sinful man by sending His Son to die for their sins. Romans 5:1 says, *"Therefore being justified by faith, we have peace with God through our Lord Jesus Christ."* And Colossians 1:20 tells us that Jesus *"made peace through the blood of His cross."* The only way we could have peace with God is through the blood of His cross. That is how God "atoned" for our sins.

The work of Christ for us is called the *atonement*. That word can be broken up into several parts to say *"at-one-ment"* instead of *atonement*, revealing a central part of its meaning. Having peace with God means, in part, being *"at one"* with God. We, who were

[43] Please see Chapter 5 "Repent and Believe" for more information on receiving salvation.
[44] To reconcile means to make peace. Before salvation people are not at peace with God; they are enemies of God (Romans 5:10) and need peace with God.

the enemies of God are, through the sacrifice of Jesus, "at one" or "at peace" with God. This is called the *substitutionary atonement* of Christ. By dying *for* us Jesus provided peace for us with God.

In the Gospels we can read the account of Jesus' crucifixion.[45] The Romans had perfected the art of torturing criminals to death. It was a slow, agonizing way to die. Every moment was filled with unimaginable pain. And the moments went by slowly, one agonizing moment after another, for hours. For Jesus, the pain would have been especially high. His back had been torn open by the scourging whip of the Roman soldiers. His open wounds now on the cross scraped up and down against the rough wood of the cross. In order to breathe, He had to push His body up, pushing against the nails through His feet to raise Himself up enough to get a breath of air. The nails through His feet and hands caused pounding throbs of pain which swept over Him. He had been up all night under relentless trial and prosecution. He had been beaten with hands and clubs. He had been mocked and spit upon. He wore a crown of thorns which pierced His brow. He was tortured to death.

But the worst of the pain was hidden from man's view. From noon to 3 PM there was a great darkness upon the land and God the Father shielded His Son from the mockers at the foot of the cross. During this time God the Father poured out on the Son the

---

45 See Matthew 27, Mark 15, Luke 23, and John 19 for detailed accounts of the events of the crucifixion.

full measure of His wrath against *our* sin. And then came what we might assume was the worst pain of all – the pain of the eternal Son being separated from the eternal Father, as the Father turned His face away from His sin-laden Son. As the Son became sin for us[46] He was forsaken by the Father.[47] This adds special meaning to us when we realize the Lord has promised to never leave nor forsake us (Hebrews 13:5). Jesus knows what it is like to be forsaken and He promises it will never happen to those who belong to Him. He was forsaken so that we would never be.

When Jesus had finished paying for our sin, He said these final words of victory: *"It is finished"* (John 19:30). This is an expression that means "the debt is paid in full." Nothing else needed to be paid; indeed, nothing else could be paid. Jesus had made peace through the blood of His cross. Man could now be reconciled with God.

The Prophet Isaiah was used by God to speak about the suffering of our Savior for sin. He wrote these prophetic words 700 years before the birth of Christ. The cross was not the Roman's idea, nor was it the Jew's. The cross was God's plan for salvation even before the beginning of the world.[48] This is why, even in the Garden of Eden, God promised that a Deliverer would come to defeat sin and the works of Satan (Genesis 3:15). Although Isaiah

---
46 2 Corinthians 5:21.
47 Matthew 27:46; Psalm 22:1.
48 See Acts 2:23, 4:28; Ephesians 1:4-5.

gives a number of prophecies concerning the coming Messiah, the one which most directly speaks of the death of Messiah[49] is Isaiah 53. Actually, the whole prophecy runs from Isaiah 52:13 through Isaiah 53:12, and consists of 5 stanza's[50] which contain 3 verses each: *1)* 52:13-15, *2)* 53:1-3, *3)* 53:4-6, *4)* 53:7-9, *5)* 53:10-12. The whole passage is written in Hebrew poetry. Usually, in this kind of poetic structure it is the "middle" stanza which is the central or main idea of the passage. In this case, that would be Isaiah 53:4-6. Here are those verses:

⁴ Surely he hath borne our griefs, and carried our sorrows: yet we did esteem him stricken, smitten of God, and afflicted. ⁵ But he was wounded for our transgressions, he was bruised for our iniquities: the chastisement of our peace was upon him; and with his stripes we are healed. ⁶ All we like sheep have gone astray; we have turned every one to his own way; and the LORD hath laid on him the iniquity of us all.

Now we will take a little bit closer look at these three verses. First of all, a general observation: notice how often the word "our" occurs in verses 4 and 5. It was for *our* griefs, *our* sorrows,

---

49 The word "Christ" in the New Testament is the Greek word for the Old Testament Hebrew word "Messiah."

50 Hymns are divided into verses. We could also call those hymn verses "stanzas." In a poem, like Isaiah 53, each stanza is like a verse in a hymn.

our transgressions, ***our*** iniquities and ***our*** peace that Jesus was crucified. This reminds us of the substitutionary nature of His suffering and death. It was in ***our*** place; it was instead of us; it was for us.

Here are some specific observations from these verses. Exploring these verses in more detail means that we will be going deeper into the text. This will be a little bit more technical and difficult, but hopefully the extra concentration on the reader's part will result in the reward of clearer and deeper understanding of this marvelous text. You may also want to take off your sandals as you read these sacred verses, for this is holy ground.

1) *"**Surely** he hath borne our griefs..."* Verse 4 begins with the word "surely" which means "certainly, truly, indeed." This particular word in Hebrew is used to emphasize something which is unexpected. "Whatever people may have thought about the crucifixion and its sorrows and sufferings, the *truth* was dramatically different."[51] It was unexpected because no one would have ever expected God to nail His Son to a cross for our sins!

2) *"Surely **he** hath borne our griefs..."* The word *"he"* (which refers to Jesus) in these verses is written in such a way that it is emphasized.[52] In other words, this is like Isaiah saying of the Messiah

---

51 J. Alec Motyer, The Prophecy of Isaiah, (InterVarsity Press, Downers Grove, IL) 1993, pg. 430.

52 In Hebrew the pronouns (like "he") are most often incorporated into the verb itself. In fact, we often find both the subject and the object of the verb as part of the verb. But when the writer wanted to draw special attention to the

that *"he himself has borne our griefs"* emphasizing the personal and purposeful nature of Jesus' sacrifice.

3) *"Surely he **hath borne** our griefs..."* This means literally that Jesus "lifted up" our griefs from us in order to take them away. Our griefs are the things which cause us sorrow. They are like a heavy burden we carry. Jesus came to lift them off of us and take them away.

4) *"Surely he hath borne **our griefs**..."* Jesus Himself was described as *"despised and rejected of men; a man of sorrows, and acquainted with grief"* in the previous verse (Isaiah 53:3). The things which cause us grief[53] Jesus has lifted up or "borne" on the cross. A person might say, "But I still have grief and sickness in this life." That is true. But remember that the final fulfillment of *all* the benefits of what Jesus did on the cross will not be realized or experienced until we get to heaven. There will be no more sickness there! Matthew saw this prophecy as being partly fulfilled during Jesus' earthly ministry of healing thousands of people.[54]

5) "...*and **carried** our sorrows*" The word *carried* means "to bear a load or a burden." Specifically, He took up the burden of our sorrows.[55] Jesus

---

pronoun, he would add it in again as a separate word. That is what has been done in these verses.

53 This word "grief" refers to any kind of sickness or disease which cause great distress.

54 See Matthew 8:16-17. Through His healing ministry Jesus was showing the "firstfruits" of what He would win on the cross.

55 The word "sorrows" refers to pains caused by infirmity, mental or physical anguish.

> *"Surely he hath borne our griefs*
> *and carried our sorrows..."*

invites us to bring our burdens and sorrows to Him (Matthew 11:28-30).

6) *"yet we did esteem him stricken, smitten of God, and afflicted"* Here is where mankind, and especially His executioners and mockers got things, backwards. It *seemed* as if Jesus was suffering for His own sin and was being punished by God. The people at the foot of the cross thought that Jesus was forsaken by God (and they were right!). The crowd cried out, *"He saved others, He cannot save Himself"* (and they were right!). They thought Jesus was being punished for sin (and they were right!). But you might think *"surely something else was going on"* (and you are right!). Jesus was forsaken by God and paying for sin – not His sin, but *our* sin. Jesus could not come down from the cross and save Himself because His love for us and His obedience to the Father, even to death on the cross, held Him there more than the nails ever could have. He was determined to pay for our sin and He stayed on the cross until our every sin was covered by the blood of His sacrifice.

Verse 5: *"But he was wounded for our transgressions, he was bruised for our iniquities: the chastisement of our peace was upon him; and with his stripes we are healed."*

7) *"**But**..."* This word, which indicates a contrast, alerts us to the fact that indeed something different was going on than what people might have thought.

8) ***"he was wounded** for our transgressions"* The word "wounded" is actually much stronger than it seems. We think of a wound as perhaps a cut or bruise that is bad but will heal. However, the Hebrew word means "to pierce through" or "to fatally wound." It can even mean "to bore a hole through" something. In the Bible it is most often used of a death wound delivered to a dragon or monster![56]

9) *"he was wounded **for our transgressions**..."* The word "for" means "resulting from" or "because of," so we could translate this as *"he was wounded because of our transgressions."* This is a reminder that the *reason* Jesus had to suffer on the cross was because of our sin. The word *"transgressions"* means sin that is purposeful and rebellious against God. It reminds us that our sin is a deliberate[57] revolt against the Lord and His Holy Law.

"he was wounded for our transgressions..."
"he was bruised for our iniquities..."

10) *"he was **bruised** for our iniquities..."* Like the word "wounded" at the beginning of this verse, the word "bruised" does not describe (in modern English) the depth or extreme degree of the Hebrew word it translates. Instead of "bruised" as we commonly

---

56 See Isaiah 51:9 for an example.
57 "Deliberate" means something that is done on purpose. We do not sin by accident; we sin because we want to.

think of it, the meaning was more like "crushed" or "broken" or "beaten to pieces." Our Savior was crushed by the weight of our sins and the wrath of God.

11) *"he was bruised **for our iniquities**..."* The word *"iniquities"* refers to something that is "bent" in a wrong way, something (or someone!) who is depraved and perverse.[58] This is talking about our sin nature which is "bent" always toward sinning. We have a bent toward sin and we are bent on sinning. A rifle with a bent barrel will not shoot straight no matter how good the intentions are of the person shooting. This is why we "miss the mark" in our lives. Our whole lives, by nature, are bent in the wrong direction. Jesus was crushed ***"for our"*** (because of our) bent toward sin.[59] This serves as yet another reminder of the substitutionary nature of Christ's death. It was in our place.

12) *"the chastisement of our peace was upon him..."* The word *"chastisement"* means correction, discipline, or punishment. A parent will "chastise," or correct a child when they do wrong. Yet Jesus did no wrong. He suffered for all the wrong that we have done. Whatever punishment we deserved was placed on our Savior. The punishment that was required to bring about our peace with God fell on Jesus. He gained peace for us *"by the blood of His cross"* (Colossians 1:20).

---

58 "Perverse" means to be turned away from that which is right or good. It is like the word "corrupt."
59 See Ephesians 2:1-3 concerning our natural bent toward sin.

13) *"...and with his stripes we are healed."* The word *"stripes"* here most likely refers to the cuts inflicted by the scourging at the hand of the Roman soldiers. The healing spoken of here means the final and total healing all believers will experience one day. We think naturally of physical healing, but this would include more importantly spiritual healing, and in addition emotional and psychological healing. This is healing of the total person. In Heaven we will suffer no more because He suffered in our place. *"the chastisement of our peace was upon him..."*

Verse 6 *"All we like sheep have gone astray; we have turned every one to his own way; and the LORD hath laid on him the iniquity of us all."*

14) *"**All we** like sheep have gone astray..."* In the Hebrew text, this verse actually begins and ends with the same words: *all we*. This is a reminder that everyone is included. All of us are guilty. *"For all have sinned, and come short of the glory of God"* (Romans 3:23). All of us are guilty sheep and we, by our sin, have caused the death of our Great Shepherd.

15) *"All we **like sheep have gone astray**"* We have lived like foolish sheep, going astray and in danger of eternal lostness. We have been wandering in the darkness and in the spiritual desert. By going *"astray"* we have gone *away from* the Lord, our Shepherd. A sinner has his back toward God and is walking, sometimes running, into the darkness.

16) *"...we have turned every one to his own way..."* Having ignored or rejected the Lord's way, all of us (every one) have instead turned to our own way. *"There is a way which seems right unto a man, but the end thereof are the ways of death"* (Proverbs 14:12).

All of us are guilty sheep and we,
by our sin, have caused the death of
our Great Shepherd.

17) *"...and the LORD hath laid on him the iniquity of us all."* The punishment of all our sin and rebellion against God had to be paid. There are only two options: 1) we could pay for it ourselves by suffering in hell for eternity (which even then would never completely pay the debt), or 2) we could accept the gift of eternal life (Romans 6:23) offered to us because Jesus fully paid the debt of our guilt. God did not owe us Option 2. All of us deserve nothing more than Option 1. It is only by God's great grace and everlasting love that He not only offers Option 2, He *"laid on him the iniquity of us all."* That means God, the Lord, laid, or put, on Jesus all of our sin. God the Father took all of our sin, all of our guilt, and He laid it on God the Son while He was on the cross. The full and eternal wrath of God was poured out on our Savior.

18) *"...and **the LORD hath laid on him** the iniquity of us all."* There is one more important detail to notice in the verse. The Hebrew verb translated *"hath laid"* is in a form that means God *caused* all of our sin to land on Christ.[60] The verb itself means something like "to arrive at" or "to make to meet."[61] If, for example, you were to bring one end of a rope to "arrive at" or "meet" the other end of a rope, then you could cause them to be joined together in a knot. So the idea of this verse is that God caused our sin to meet Jesus on the cross.

> *"...and the LORD hath laid on him the iniquity of us all."*

19) If we skip down to verse 10 in the chapter (Isaiah 53), we again see that this was God's purpose or will: He caused it to happen because He wanted Jesus to die on the cross for our sin. The first part of verse 10 says, *"Yet it pleased the LORD to bruise him; he hath put him to grief."* Here is a remarkable statement: *"...it **pleased** the Lord to bruise him."* The word *"pleased"* here refers to not only being willing for something to happen, but rather to be delighted or very happy that something happened! God was glad to crush His Son! Why? How could that be? First of all, we must admit that God's ways are past our finding out or figuring out (Romans 11:33) and, as God led Isaiah to write two chapters after this one: *"For my thoughts are not your thoughts, neither are your ways my ways, says the LORD. ⁹ For as the heavens are higher than the*

---

60 It is in the Hiphil form which is causative. This is the way Hebrew changes a verb from its normal meaning to instead emphasize that something was caused to happen. This usually (as here) indicates it was done on purpose.
61 Motyer, The Prophecy of Isaiah, pg. 431.

earth, so are my ways higher than your ways, and my thoughts than your thoughts" (Isaiah 55:8-9). Yet we are not without some understanding, as limited as that may be. It helps if we consider this from heaven's point of view instead of an earthly point of view, if we try to see it in light of eternity. It pleased the Father to do this because He knew that this was the only way for us to be saved. It was His plan from the beginning.[62] God is always pleased when His will is done.

In the cross of Christ, the will of God was fully accomplished. That pleased the Father. But there is more involved. It was also pleasing to God to cause the very thing that would enable us to have eternal life. God, Who is all-knowing and all-wise, saw from His eternal, heavenly point of view all of those who would one day come to have a right relationship with Him through faith in the saving work of the Son, and this pleased Him.

God also knew the glory which He would receive in eternity to come. Those who would be saved would praise and glorify Him forever.[63] That was pleasing to the Father. In a similar way, the writer of Hebrews says, *"Looking unto Jesus the author and finisher of our faith;* **who for the joy that was set before him endured the cross,** *despising the shame, and is set down at the right hand of the throne of God"* (Hebrews 12:2, emphasis added). We would certainly not count it as "joy" to endure the cross! But Jesus, exactly like the Father, knew the trophies of His grace that

---

62 See Acts 2:23 and Acts 4:28. God predetermined the crucifixion of Jesus. He had a definite plan which could not be changed by anyone or anything.
63 See, for example, Ephesians 1:12 and 2:7.

would come as a result. This, therefore, is what Jesus did to pay the price for our ransom from sin, to deliver us from hell, to save our souls and to bring us to heaven. May we glorify Him forever, including right now.

"...it pleased the Lord to bruise him."

STUDY QUESTIONS FOR CHAPTER 4

1. Give three verses which tell us that Jesus never sinned:
   a)
   b)
   c)

2. Jesus, by His sacrifice for us, took away our _____ and gave us His _____
(2 Corinthians 5:21).

3. Jesus was our "substitute sacrifice." What does the word "substitute" mean?

And how does it apply to the idea of Jesus' sacrifice for us?

4. Jesus made the "atonement" for our sins. What does the word "atonement" mean?

5. Read Isaiah 53:4-6 several times. What is it in that passage that really speaks to your heart?

6. Isaiah 53:10 says that it *"pleased the LORD to bruise Him…"* Explain why that is true.

Chapter 5

Receiving Salvation: Repent & Believe

Jesus began His ministry by saying *"The time is fulfilled, and the kingdom of God is at hand: **repent ye, and believe the gospel**"* (Mark 1:15).

Paul said that he continually and faithfully taught "repentance toward God, and faith toward our Lord Jesus Christ" (Acts 20:21).

> *Salvation is free*
> *But it is not cheap!*
> *It cost Jesus <u>everything</u>*

Salvation is a gift from God.[64] It is free to us, but it was very costly to God. The price He paid was the death of His Son on the cross. That is how God "so loved the world." And now God offers this free gift to sinners, to His enemies,[65] to those who have rebelled against Him and His rule. This precious gift is freely offered, but it also must be received. How do people "receive" this gift of salvation? The purpose of this chapter is to answer that important question.

Imagine if someone brought you a gift and offered it to you.

---
64 Ephesians 2:8-9; Romans 6:23; John 3:16
65 Romans 5:10

The gift is wrapped up in a box and you cannot tell what is inside. It might be a million dollars, or it might be a bomb! Would you accept that gift? Would you "receive" or "take" the gift? It would probably depend on who is offering the gift to you. If it is a complete stranger, you might, wisely, be reluctant to take it. But if it is someone you trust, someone who loves you, then you would gladly receive it.

In addition to offering sinful people this amazing gift of salvation through Jesus, God does something else: He makes us ready to receive His gift by opening our spiritual understanding so that we are able to see 1) how bad our sin is, and 2) how great His love is. Then we are prepared to receive the gift.

The Bible speaks of salvation as "conversion." A person is "saved" by being "converted." The words "conversion" and "converted" basically mean "to turn back." In Acts 3:19 the Apostle Peter preached: *"Repent ye therefore, and be converted, that your sins may be blotted out, when the times of refreshing shall come from the presence of the Lord."* This means that a person needs to "be converted" so that their sins "may be blotted out" (wiped out or erased). Since this is true, we need to know what it means to be converted.

There are two parts or two "sides" to conversion. One is "believe" and the other is "repent." One does not exist without the other. These two sides, believing and repenting, are like the two sides to the same coin. You might focus on one side or the other, but both sides are always there and both sides are equally necessary.

The reason why conversion has two sides is because it refers to two things which happen together. We turn away from sin and we turn to Jesus at the same time. The turning away from sin is called repentance and the turning to Jesus is called faith (believe, belief).[66]

An unsaved person has his back toward God, and is facing toward sin and moving in that direction. A saved person has his back toward sin, and is facing toward God and moving in that direction. There are no other options. Either your face is toward God or your back is toward God, and just as true, either your face is toward sin or your back is toward sin. You cannot be going two directions at the same time; neither can you follow sin and follow God at the same time.[67]

Jesus said that people need to *repent* and *believe* the gospel.[68] Those are the two parts of conversion. Both repentance and faith are required. Simply put, repentance means saying "no" to sin; faith means saying "yes" to God. That is a basic, beginning definition of repentance and faith, but as we shall see, the Bible has much more to say about these two topics.

---

66 Both *faith* and *believe* come from the same Greek word. Depending on the context it might be translated either way. To have faith means to believe.
67 This does not mean that a saved person never sins (1 John 1:8-10), but the direction of his life is toward God and away from sin.
68 Mark 1:15

REPENTANCE

Repentance happens because God grants or gives it to us. For instance, when the Apostles (who were Jewish) realized that God was working in the hearts of the Gentiles (the non-Jewish people), they said, *"Then hath God also to the Gentiles **granted** repentance unto life"* (Acts 11:18).[69] Paul reminds us of God's purpose in His patience and goodness to sinners: *"Or despisest[70] thou the riches of his goodness and forbearance and longsuffering; not knowing that **the goodness of God leads thee to repentance?** (Romans 2:4).* Notice that the goodness of God leads us to repentance (Romans 2:4) and repentance leads to spiritual life (Acts 11:18).

What does "repentance" mean? How does a person repent? The Bible uses several different words to talk about repentance. One of those words means "to turn back." The idea is of a person who is going in the direction of sin and needs to "turn back" or turn around and go the opposite direction. The sinner is going the wrong way, a way that leads to disaster and eternal death, and he or she must turn back before it is too late.

A young man was working for a construction company, building a high bridge. He worked on that bridge day after day. One evening after work he went out drinking with some friends. Even

---

[69] See also Acts 5:31, Acts 3:19 and 2 Timothy 2:25. Repentance is granted (given) by God, that is, He works in us to bring us to repentance. When we repent it is a reaction to what God is doing inside of us, in our spirit.

[70] The word "despise" here means "to think little of something" or to take something lightly, as if it is not important.

though he was drunk, this young man decided he could drive himself home. So he got into his car and headed in the direction that seemed most normal to him – he headed toward the unfinished bridge. Tragically, his car went flying off the unfinished end of that bridge, fell to the ground below and burst into flames. The young man died that night. He thought he was going in the right direction. He thought he was safe. He thought he was on his way home. He needed someone to tell him that he was going in the wrong direction; that the way he was going would lead to certain death. The young man needed to turn back. He needed to turn around before it was too late. That is what repentance is – it is God telling us that we need to turn around, that we need to turn back from sin before it leads to a tragic end. When a person responds with obedience to this inward call of God to turn away from sin that means they have repented.

The reason the "good news" of the gospel is so good is because the "bad news" of sin is so bad. In presenting the gospel we should make clear *what* a person is being saved *from*. Why does a person need to be saved? Because if they do not turn away from sin (and turn to God)[71] the cost or the payment for that sin is eternal death![72]

---

[71] Even though we are talking about repentance here instead of "faith" remember that they can never really be separated. A person turns away from sin but at the same time turns toward God. Our only purpose in separating them in this discussion is to focus on the meaning of each term by itself.
[72] Romans 6:23; Ezekiel 18:4, 20.

Another Bible word for repentance means "to change one's mind." The first word we talked about means to change your direction; this word means to change your mind (or thinking). This change of mind has specially to do with Jesus Christ. *What* is a person changing his or her mind about in repentance? The emphasis in the New Testament is that a change in how one thinks of Jesus has to take place. At one point we did not think of Him as Savior and Lord, and so we needed to change our thinking, our mind, and agree that what the Bible says about Jesus is true. Both faith and repentance are based on God's truth as given to us in the Bible.

On the Day of Pentecost (Acts 2), God used the Apostle Peter to preach the gospel. As we read this passage (Acts 2:1-38), it becomes evident that Peter's emphasis in his message is on *who* Jesus is. Peter especially makes it clear that Jesus is more than a man or a prophet; Jesus is God and He is risen from the dead. Peter ends his message by saying, *"Therefore let all the house of Israel know assuredly, that God hath made that same Jesus, whom ye have crucified, both Lord and Christ"* (Acts 2:36). Jesus is the Christ (Messiah) and He is also Lord! The Jews had rejected Jesus. They did not think of Jesus as the Messiah and they especially did not think that Jesus was the Lord. They needed to change their mind about this crucial truth. So the people were *"pricked (cut) in their heart"* (vs 37) and asked, *"What shall we do?"* Peter answered their question by saying, *"Repent..."* (change your mind). They needed to agree with the truth that Jesus Christ is Lord.

Another sermon by Peter is recorded for us in Acts 3:1-26. There again Peter taught the people about the glory of who Jesus is. In addition to Jesus being Lord and Messiah, Peter said Jesus was the Holy One (vs 14), the Just (righteous), and the Prince (author) of life (vs 15). Peter also said that the people had been thinking about Jesus the wrong way. In verse 17 he said that he knew it was *"through ignorance* (lack of knowledge)[73] *ye did it, as did also your rulers."* Yet ignorance is not an excuse. Once we know the truth, we must also believe the truth and base our life and our decisions on the truth. When Peter finished this message on the truth of who Jesus is and what He did he ended by saying, *"Repent ye therefore, and be converted, that your sins may be blotted out..."* (Acts 3:19). In order for their sins to be blotted out they needed to first of all "repent" or "change their thinking" about Jesus.

The Christian life is first of all and most of all about Christ.

---

[73] The word translated "ignorance" here is not talking about how smart someone is; it is talking about someone who is literally "without knowledge" of the truth about who Jesus is. Therefore, their knowledge, or thinking, had to change. They had to "repent" of their wrong ideas about Jesus and accept the truth about Him.

It is true that repentance must be about sin. But it is also first and primarily true that repentance is about *who Jesus is*. It is only because of the greatness of who Jesus *is* that He was able to do what He did to save us.[74] One of the reasons so many churches and believers have such a weak faith is that they mistakenly think the Christian life is primarily about them and their salvation. There is something even more important than that and we dare not miss it. The Christian life is first of all and most of all about Christ. When Paul wrote to the Corinthians and reminded them about his message to them he said it was about *"Jesus Christ and Him crucified"* (1 Corinthians 2:2). His message was not just "salvation" – it was "Jesus" because without Jesus there is no salvation. Paul said that he *"preached Jesus"* – that was his message.[75] Once people come to see the truth about who Jesus is then, and not till then, they are ready to hear the truth about the gospel (1 Corinthians 15:1-4).

Repentance requires changing our thinking about Jesus. This is because at one point in time we did not think of Him (or glorify Him) as Lord and Savior, and now, coming to know the truth about Him, we do.

Repentance is also about changing our mind concerning *sin*. We at one time *"served sin"* (Romans 6:17, 20). We lived for sin, which is another way of saying we lived for *self*. Paul said of himself and of all of us, *"For we ourselves also were sometimes foolish, disobedient,*

---

[74] Therefore, we have included two chapters in this book devoted to the topics of "Who Jesus Is" and "What Jesus Did" near the beginning of this book (see chapters 3 and 4).
[75] See 2 Corinthians 4:5; Colossians 1:28; Acts 17:3.

deceived, serving divers (different) *lusts and pleasures, living in malice and envy, hateful, and hating one another"* (Titus 3:3). We are as guilty as other sinners in this world *"among whom also **we all** had our conversation* (way of living) *in times past in the lusts of our flesh, fulfilling the desires of the flesh and of the mind; and **were by nature the children of wrath, even as others**"* (Ephesians 2:3, emphasis added). Both by nature and by choice we lived for sin.

Even though we have sinned against God all of our lives, God still showed His love to us by sending His Son to die for us – for our sins (Romans 5:8). In fact, we were worse than sinners. We were the enemies of God![76]

God not only sent His Son to pay the price for our sin, He also sent the Holy Spirit to convict the world of sin, righteousness and judgment.[77] The Holy Spirit opens our spiritual eyes to at last be able to see the truth. Remember that unsaved people are spiritually dead. Dead people cannot see anything, much less respond to anything. Therefore, the Holy Spirit "quickens"[78] spiritually dead people so that they can finally see what they have never been able to see before – spiritual truth about Jesus, sin, righteousness and judgment. The effect of this "reviving" work of

---

76 Romans 6:10. This is why we needed "peace" with God, which verse 1 of the same chapter says is ours "having been justified by faith."

77 See John 16:8-10. In addition, the Holy Spirit was also sent to glorify Christ (vs 14).

78 The KJV word "quicken" means to "make alive" or "revive" (see John 6:44, 63, 65; Ephesians 2:1 and 5; Colossians 2:13).

the Holy Spirit is that we can see spiritual truth (our great need of forgiveness from sin and God's great gift in Jesus Christ and His sacrifice) and respond with repentance.

Repenting from sin means turning *away* from sin, it means saying "no" to sin. Repenting from sin will often be accompanied by a sorrow for sin.[79] But repentance is more than just being sorry. There is a story of a Sunday School teacher who asked her young class what was meant by the word "repent." One little boy said, "it means being sorry for your sins." Then a little girl said, "It is more than that; it is being sorry enough to *quit*!" There is a lot of truth to that. A person who truly repents will not only be sorry for sin, but will also turn away from sin.

BELIEVE

Repentance, as we have seen, means turning away from sin. Believing (having faith) means turning to God. Both repentance and faith happen together. They are two parts of the same motion. We have spent most of this chapter discussing the area of repentance.[80] The other side of repentance is faith, and faith is

[79] 2 Corinthians 7:8-11 describes the difference between "worldly sorrow" and "godly sorrow." Just because a person seems to be "sorry" does not mean that person has repented.

[80] The reason for spending most of the chapter on "repentance" rather than "faith" is because repentance is less understood and less taught in general than faith. Most people have heard many messages on faith but few, if any, on repentance. Also, faith is an easier idea to grasp. The lack of space here in the chapter is not meant to say that faith is less important than repentance. Faith is essential to the Christian life! Romans 1:17; Hebrews 1:6.

based on the same truths we learned about regarding repentance.

Saving faith is specifically about Jesus Christ – who Jesus is and what Jesus did for our salvation. Saving faith is based on the gospel truth as given to us in the Bible. We do not have faith in "faith" but we have faith in *Jesus Christ* as He is revealed in the unchanging truth of God's Word. Saving faith is all of me (my mind, will and heart) receiving and trusting in all of Jesus (the saving work of His sacrificial death, burial and resurrection, and His Rule or Lordship over all). With all I am, I trust in all He is and all He has done to save me.

> *Natural fiath "hopes,"*
> *but biblical faith "knows."*

The biblical use of the word "faith" always refers to something which is *certain*.[81] Sometimes in our day people use the word "faith" to talk about things which are not certain, things which people might *hope* for or wish to be true. For example, a person might say, "I have great faith that our team is going to win the game," or, "I believe in our team." Used that way, faith means simply having positive thoughts or hopes. There always remains a level of uncertainty with that kind of faith. But biblical, saving faith is based on what is true, sure, unchanging, and certain because it is based on the perfect Word of God. Natural faith

---

81 See, for instance, Hebrews 11:1.

"hopes," but biblical faith "knows."

Because saving faith is founded on the certainty of God's truth, having faith really means to *trust*. By faith we put our *trust* in God. The level of trust we have is based on the faithfulness and character of the one we are trusting. If someone is not dependable, you will not likely trust what he or she says. God is perfect in all His ways[82] and God is completely dependable. We can safely and fully trust in Him. *"Thy word is true from the beginning: and every one of thy righteous judgments endures* (lasts) *for ever"* (Psalm 119:160).

A man decides to sit in the chair because he trusts (he believes, or has faith) that the chair is trustworthy. He can "rest" in the chair because he is sure it will hold him up. If the man said, "I have faith the chair will hold me up," but he never sat in it, we would wonder if he really "believed" in the chair at all. But when he actually *sits* in the chair, he proves that he trusts the chair to hold him up. Saving faith is similar to that. It is not enough to simply say, "I believe in Jesus Christ." If we *really* believe in Him we will completely trust in Him; trusting both in Who He is (Lord) and what He has done (Savior).

When the New Testament talks about faith in connection to salvation, it almost always connects that faith specifically to the Lord Jesus Christ. It was Jesus who died for our sins and was

---

[82] Psalm 18:30

raised from the dead.[83] It is not enough to believe in "God" in a general way. The Bible says we are to specifically believe in Jesus Christ. "Neither is there salvation in any other: for there is none other name under heaven given among men, whereby we must be saved" (Acts 4:12). Jesus said, "I am the way, the truth, and the life: no man cometh unto the Father, but by me" (John 14:6).

In the story of the Philippian jailer (Acts 16:25-34), the jailer asked Paul and Silas, *"What must I do to be saved"* (Acts 16:30). That is a great question! That is a question we wish every person in the world would ask. Notice that the jailer thought he had to "do" something to be saved. That is our natural tendency, to think that we *should* do something and to believe that we *can* do something to earn salvation. But Paul doesn't spend time correcting this man's wrong theology. He simply states the truth: *"Believe on the Lord Jesus Christ, and thou shalt be saved, and thy house"* (verse 31). Believe = have faith in = trust in the Lord Jesus Christ.

> *Having faith in Jesus Christ means fully trusting in who He is and what He has done in providing salvation for us.*

The Apostle Paul said that his constant message was *"testifying both to the Jews, and also to the Greeks, **repentance toward God**, and **faith toward our Lord Jesus Christ**"* (Acts 20:21). He also wrote

---

83 In fact, that is what the Gospel is about – the death, burial and resurrection of Jesus Christ. See Chapter One of this book and 1 Corinthians 15:1-4.

to the Galatians, *"A man is not justified by the works of the law, but by **the faith of Jesus Christ**, even we have **believed in Jesus Christ**, that we might be **justified by the faith of Christ**, and not by the works of the law: for by the works of the law shall no flesh be justified"* (Galatians 2:16, emphasis added).[84] Having faith in Jesus Christ means fully trusting in who He is and what He has done in providing salvation for us. Because Jesus is Lord, and because He died on the cross to pay the penalty for our sins, He is able to save all who put their trust in Him.[85]

Since the idea of *trusting* is so important in saving faith we should think a little bit more about what it means to *trust*. There is an old story about a famous tightrope walker named Walanda. He would stretch a rope from one high point to another high point and walk from one side to the other on the rope, high above the ground. One day, Walanda stretched his rope across a canyon, hundreds of feet above the ground. If he fell off the rope, it would mean certain death. As crowds gathered and cheered on both sides of the canyon, he began his journey walking on the rope. When he reached the other side all the people cheered and clapped their hands. Walanda asked the people, "Do you believe I can do it again?" All the people said "Yes, we believe you can do it!" This time Walanda used a wheelbarrow and pushed the

---
84 Also see Romans 3:22-26, 5:1; Galatians 3:26; Ephesians 3:17; Philippians 3:9; Colossians 1:4, 2:5; 2 Timothy 3:15
85 John 6:37-40; Romans 10:8-13

wheelbarrow in front of him on the rope all the way across the canyon. The people cheered even more loudly. Walanda then asked if they believed he could cross the canyon again, this time with <u>someone inside</u> the wheelbarrow. The people shouted, *"Yes, we believe you can do it!"* Walanda then asked, *"If you believe I can cross the canyon with a person inside the wheelbarrow, <u>who</u> will get inside?"* This last question Walanda asked shows the difference between merely "believing" something and what it means to "trust" something. All the people said they believed, but only someone who *really trusted* would be willing to get inside the wheelbarrow. It would mean trusting Walanda with their life!

A lot of people say they believe in God. Only those who *trust* God with their lives and with their eternal destiny have biblical faith. Having faith that Jesus is Lord and He is Savior means trusting in Jesus *alone* (and not works or anything or anyone else). Only Jesus can save.

To believe something is true is a matter of the *mind*. It is based on what we think is true. But when we talk about trust, something more than our mind is involved. Trust is also a matter of the *will* of a person. Whenever you *trust* you make a decision. Saving faith is more than just knowing the story of Jesus. It is more than just believing those facts about Jesus to be true. Even the demons believe that everything about Jesus is real and true! We have to start by believing the truth about Jesus with our mind.

But that belief must also reach our *will*. We must make a *decision* to trust in Jesus, and to trust in Him alone.

There is a third part to saving faith. We have talked about the mind and the will, now at last we must add the heart. The Bible often uses the word "heart" to talk about our innermost being – who we really are inside. If you tell someone you love, *"I love you with all my mind,"* that will not be as meaningful to them as saying, *"I love you with all my heart."* The heart includes what we think but it also includes much more because it is *personal*. I might believe that $2 + 2 = 4$, but I have no personal commitment to it. So it is with saving faith; it goes beyond simply believing facts about Christ to having a deep personal commitment *to Christ*. Jesus Himself told us that the greatest commandment is, *"Thou shalt love the Lord thy God with all thy heart, and with all thy soul, and with all thy mind"* (Matthew 22:37). This is what makes Christianity so different and so special. It is not about a religion; it is about a relationship – a very personal relationship with God through Jesus Christ. Truly loving Jesus proves we have a relationship with God (John 8:47).

Biblical, saving faith is more than just knowing and believing, it is even more than just making a decision. It also includes *loving* the Lord your God with all your heart, with all your soul and with all your mind (Matthew 22:37). As you read the following verses from Romans 10, notice the connection between believing and the heart.

"If thou shalt confess with thy mouth the Lord Jesus, and shalt believe in thine heart that God hath raised him from the dead, thou shalt be saved. ¹⁰For with the heart man believeth unto righteousness; and with the mouth confession is made unto salvation. ¹¹ For the scripture saith, Whosoever believeth on him shall not be ashamed. ¹² For there is no difference between the Jew and the Greek: for the same Lord over all is rich unto all that call upon him. ¹³For whosoever shall call upon the name of the Lord shall be saved" (Romans 10:9-13).

Our Lord uses very tender words about believers. We are called His sheep, brothers (and sisters) friends, beloved, family, loved ones, and bride, just to name a few. God is love[86] and He calls us into a loving relationship with Him. We have the calling and the privilege to do more than merely believe in Him and trust in Him. We have the blessing of loving Him and being loved by Him. Every belief system man has come up with involves some measure of faith, but only in Christianity do we find the blessing of relationship with God. That is because there is only one true God. All other false gods and idols are only ideas and fakes. They are not personal because they are not real. There is no way to have a personal relationship with an idol or a pretend god. But the one true God is a personal God who desires to have a person-

---
[86] See 1 John 4:7-16 where John speaks of the truth of God's love and also of what our love should be like.

al relationship with His people for eternity. The Lord God says, *"Yea, I have loved thee with an everlasting love: therefore with lovingkindness have I drawn thee"* (Jeremiah 31:1). This is why God said He would write His New Covenant on the *hearts* of His people.[87]

CONCLUSION

God offers the gift of salvation, eternal life, through Jesus Christ our Lord (Romans 6:23). By faith alone in Christ alone we reach out and receive this gift. Faith is the hand that reaches up to receive the gift of salvation.

Conversion means a person has turned away from their sin (repentance) and has at the same time turned to Christ (faith). As the person turns to Christ they are given the gift of eternal life. All of this is done by the grace of God, by the power of the Spirit and to the glory of Christ. One day we will join the singing in heaven and we will sing this song: *"And they sung a new song, saying, Thou art worthy to take the book, and to open the seals thereof: for thou wast slain, and hast redeemed us to God by thy blood out of every kindred, and tongue, and people, and nation"* (Revelation 5:9).

---

87 See Jeremiah 31:31-33 and also 2 Corinthians 3:3-6.

STUDY QUESTIONS FOR CHAPTER 5

1. There are two sides to conversion. One is _____ and the other is _____.

2. The word "conversion" means "to turn back" or "turn away."
   a) What is a person turning away *from*?

   b) What is a person turning *to*?

3. The main New Testament word for "repentance" means "to change one's mind."
   What is a person supposed to change his mind *about*?

4. "The Christian life is first of all and most of all about _____."

5. Biblical faith involves a person's mind, will, and heart.
    a) How does faith involve a person's mind?

    b) How does faith involve a person's will?

    c) How does faith involve a person's heart?

Chapter 6

Faith and Works

If you build a fire out of pieces of wood, that fire will produce heat and light. If you told a friend, "Look at my fire" and all your friend saw was just a pile of wood with no heat and no light, your friend would not believe you had a real fire. That friend might even tell you that you were not making any sense in what you said. "How can you have a fire without also having heat and light from that fire?" your friend would ask.[88]

True faith produces good works. If you tell a friend you have faith in Jesus, and yet your friend does not see any evidence of it in the way you live, they would have reason to doubt what you say. "How can you have faith in Jesus without also having a life that shows it?" your friend would ask. How can there be a fire without light and heat?

True faith in Jesus Christ always leads to a life that is changed. Faith produces works. No one is saved by good works. But at the same time no one who is saved will lack good works. That doesn't mean a saved person never sins. But it does mean that a saved person will live in a way that shows he now belongs to the Lord

---

[88] That is the same kind of question James 2:14-26 asks. We will examine that passage later in this chapter.

Jesus Christ. According to Jesus, good trees produce good fruit.[89]

In this chapter we will see 1) a person is saved by faith and not by good works, 2) a person who has faith will also have good works as a result of his or her faith, and 3) a person who does not have good works does not have real faith. Keep in mind throughout this discussion that what we mean by a person having "faith" is not some kind of faith in faith itself but personal faith in the Person of Jesus Christ and the finished work of Jesus Christ.[90]

A PERSON IS SAVED BY FAITH
AND NOT BY WORKS

First of all, it is very clear from a number of New Testament passages that by God's grace a person is saved by faith and not by works. We will consider just a few of those passages here.

1. Romans 3 and 4

In Romans chapter 3 we see that no one deserves to be saved. No one is worthy of salvation because no one is without sin. There is *"none righteous, no not one"* and there is *"none who seeks after God"*[91] In fact, Romans 3:23 says that *"all have sinned, and come short of the glory of God."* Since no one is righteous and no one is without

---
89 Matthew 7:17-18.
90 See especially the previous chapter on "Repent and Believe" and the two chapters on "Salvation in Jesus."
91 See Romans 3:9-12 where these truths are repeated in various ways.

sin, no one can say "based on my works I deserve to be saved." If we got what we deserved, we would be in hell right now! *"For the wages of sin is death..."* (Romans 6:23). It is impossible for a person to be saved by their works because 1) we could never do enough good to make up for the bad we have done, 2) to sin in any part of the law means to be guilty of the whole law (James 2:10), and 3) even what we might call "good" is like filthy rags to God (Isaiah 64:6).

In Romans 3:22-26, Paul presents a wonderful description of how God saves us by faith in the Lord Jesus Christ. A few verses before this passage, and again in a few verses after this passage, Paul emphasizes the point that salvation is not and cannot be based on our good works:

"Therefore by the deeds of the law (by keeping the law) there shall no flesh be justified in his sight: for by the law is the knowledge of sin" (Romans 3:20). The purpose of the law is not to show us how to be saved but to show us we need to be saved. The law tells us "the knowledge of sin" (it provides the knowledge, the truth, and the proof that we have not obeyed God and have therefore sinned against God).

*"Therefore we conclude that a man is **justified by faith***

> ***without the deeds of the law"** (Romans 3:28, emphasis added). Salvation does not come from faith plus the deeds of the law (obedience). We are justified by faith without (apart from) our works.*

Having clearly stated that a person is saved by faith and not by works, Paul then turns to the example of Abraham. The Jews thought they were safe from God's judgment simply because they were the children (descendants) of Abraham.[92] Paul, in Romans 4, reminds us of what the Bible teaches about Abraham and how he became righteous in God's eyes. Paul asks if Abraham was saved by works or by faith. He then gives the answer from the Bible: *"For what saith the scripture? Abraham believed God, and it was counted unto him for righteousness"* (Romans 4:3). Paul shows by this quote from Genesis 15:6 that it was by faith (*Abraham believed God*) that Abraham was counted righteous by God.

> *"Therefore we conclude that a man is **justified by faith without the deeds of the law"** Romans 3:28*

In the verses after this Paul goes on to show 1) the difference between works and faith, 2) that Abraham was counted righteous *before* he was circumcised, and 3) that Abraham was counted righ-

---

92 See Matthew 3:9, Luke 3:8, John 8:39 and Paul's discussion of faith and Abraham in Galatians 3 and 4.

teous *before* the Law was given.[93] The conclusion from all of this is that Abraham's righteousness was *not* based on what he did and it was not based on the Law. Abraham's righteousness was based *only* on his faith. Paul then ends the chapter by showing how this relates to us today. Just like Abraham was saved by faith without works, so we also are saved by faith without works. Our faith is in "Jesus our Lord" and what He did to purchase our salvation (Romans 4:23-25). Paul then begins the next chapter with this great statement: *"Therefore **being justified by faith**, we have peace with God through our Lord Jesus Christ"* (Romans 5:1, emphasis added). By God's grace, salvation is a free gift to all who will believe in the Lord Jesus Christ. We are justified by faith and not by works.

Salvation is often spoken of as a *gift* in the New Testament.[94] In these passages, the idea of the free gift (which is not earned or deserved) is contrasted with the idea of wages (which are earned by the work a person does). Imagine that someone gives you a gift. You accept the gift and thank them. And then the person who gave the gift says, "Now you have to pay me for it." Wouldn't that destroy the whole idea of it being a gift? Or what if the giver of the gift said, "Now you have to continue to work for me every day in order to keep this gift." That would not be a gift at all! That is the same point Paul makes (especially in Romans 4) – if you think you

---

93 Paul talks about these points in Romans 4:3-16.
94 Romans 6:23; Ephesians 2:8; Romans 5:15-18; Romans 4:4-5; Acts 3:13; 2 Peter 1:1.

have to work to earn salvation or to keep your salvation, then you do not understand that salvation is a free gift!

2. Ephesians 2:8-10

"For by grace are ye saved through faith; and that not of yourselves: it is the gift of God: ⁹ Not of works, lest any man should boast. ¹⁰ For we are his workmanship, created in Christ Jesus unto good works, which God hath before ordained that we should walk in them."

This verse will be covered in more detail in Chapter 10 of this book. For now we want to consider just a few of the main points, especially regarding faith and works. First of all, this verse very clearly says that a person is *"saved through faith."*

Second, Paul says that even the faith we have is *"not of yourselves: it is the gift of God."* We cannot even take credit for the faith we have because God has given it to us, and He alone gets all the glory.[95]

Third, Paul states very clearly that we are saved *"not by works."* In other words, we are not saved by works.[96] That is a pretty clear statement that should end all questions on the matter!

Fourth, Paul then gives the reason why salvation is by faith and

[95] It is grammatically possible to understand the "gift" in this verse to apply to all the phrase "For by grace are ye saved through faith" and not only to "faith" as the gift. But either way the main point remains the same.

[96] Another very clear passage which says the same thing is Galatians 2:16.

not by works: *"lest any man should boast"* or be proud, thinking that he had some credit in salvation.

Fifth, we see from verse 10 that we are not saved *by* good works; we are saved *for* good works. Our good works do not save us, but once we are saved we should do good works. In fact, good works show that our lives have been changed by God.

> *We are not saved by good works;*
> *we are saved for good works.*

A SAVED PERSON WILL HAVE GOOD WORKS

Our next major point, that a saved person will have good works, flows from and naturally follows the first point. As we have just seen from Ephesians 2:8-10, people are not saved by works; rather, by God's grace they are saved by faith alone in Christ alone. But that is not the end of God's purpose. God also created us *for* good works. By "created" in verse 10, Paul is talking about the "new creation" that results in new life in Christ. For example, 2 Corinthians 5:17 says, *"Therefore if any man be in Christ, he is a new creature: old things are passed away; behold, all things are become new."* God has ordained[97] or decided even before our salvation what the

---

97 The word "ordained" here means "prepared beforehand," as when a person "prepares" a meal "before" a friend arrives. It is already done in advance. God does not wait to see if we are saved to prepare the works He has in mind for us; rather He knows we are going to be saved and has already prepared the good works He wants us to do. This is one of the reasons it is so important to find the Lord's will (see also Romans 12:2).

good works are that He wants us to do by His power and to His glory.[98]

Some people and churches are concerned that if we do not connect our good works to salvation then people will think that salvation only means a free ticket to heaven, and that here on earth we can do whatever we want, and live however we want. Obviously that is wrong thinking! For a person to think that once they are saved they can live for themselves instead of for God *proves* that the person does not know what it means to be saved. That person has not trusted in the Lord Jesus Christ. The answer to this problem is *not* to add a requirement for good works. Instead, the answer is 1) to make sure we believe and clearly teach the biblical gospel,[99] and 2) to show from the Bible and from the example of our lives how true saving faith leads us to do the things which please the Lord. Our character determines our actions. Who we are leads to what we do. A good tree bears good fruit.

Was the sacrifice of Jesus good enough to satisfy the righteous judgment of God?

If a person or a church adds "good works" to what is required to be saved, think about what that is saying about the sacrifice of Jesus on the cross. Was the sacrifice of Jesus good enough to satisfy the righteous

---

[98] Matthew 5:17 – Our good works should be done in a way that brings glory to God, not us.

[99] Or the gospel as it is found in the Bible. See chapter 1, The Gospel, for what is meant by "the biblical gospel."

judgment of God?[100] Would anyone dare say to Jesus, "I'm glad you died for my sins, but it just wasn't good enough!" That would be blasphemy.[101] To think that I need to add anything to what Jesus has already done is to count the blood of the covenant as an unholy or common thing (Hebrews 10:29).

Believers want to do good works, not to earn salvation, but to please the One who has saved them. True faith naturally results in good works. Again, remember that we are not talking about being perfect. This is about the *direction* of a person's life. The issue is not perfection but direction. Is the way I am living going in the direction of God and godliness?

Jesus said, *"My sheep hear my voice, and I know them, and they follow me"* (John 10:27). Someone who belongs to Jesus, the Great Shepherd, will listen to Him (*hear my voice*) and will follow Jesus in obedience.

After describing what faith *is*, Hebrews 11 talks about what faith *does*. We begin with faith because, according to Hebrews 11:6, without faith it is impossible to please God. Faith is the starting point of our relationship to God and our life for God. Faith, if it is real, always leads to the kind of life which displays faith. A mango tree proves it is a real mango tree by bearing mango fruit.

---

[100] Chapter 9 of this book discusses what is required to satisfy the wrath of God. Only the sacrificial death of Jesus could pay for our sins. Nothing else could do it, and nothing else is needed to add to it.

[101] "Blasphemy" is saying anything or thinking anything about God which is unworthy or untrue of Him.

If you pointed to a palm tree and tried to convince someone that it was really a mango tree they would have good reason to doubt you. True faith leads to good fruit.

Hebrews 11 is like a "Hall of Fame" for people of faith. The lives of people in the Old Testament who had faith in God are put on display in this chapter. What do we learn from them about faith? We learn that faith results in faithfulness; that faith leads to actions which honor God. Faith is not just something they believed, it was a way of life. Consider what God tells us about them:

1. by faith Abel *offered…* vs 4
2. by faith Noah…*prepared an ark*…vs 7
3. by faith Abraham…*obeyed and he went out*…vs 8
4. by faith Abraham *when he was tried offered up Isaac*…vs 17
5. by faith Isaac *blessed Jacob*…vs 20
6. by faith Moses…*refused to be called the son of Pharaoh's daughter; choosing rather to suffer affliction with the people of God*…vs 24-25
7. by faith they (Israel) *passed through the Red Sea*…vs 29

On and on goes the list, and with each example of faith we are told what they *did* because of their faith. Their faith is not described merely as what they believed. It is described by what they did, how they lived, how they obeyed God, even if it meant (as it often did) suffering. Also notice the order in which these descriptions of faith are listed: first we are told they had faith and then we are told how they lived *by faith*. Their faith was proven not by what they said but by what they did. Truly, *"the just shall live by faith."*[102]

So far in this chapter we have seen that 1) a person is saved by faith and not by good works and 2) a person who has faith will also have good works as a result of his or her faith. Now we are ready for our last point which is:

A PERSON WHO DOES NOT HAVE GOOD WORKS DOES NOT HAVE REAL FAITH

Works do not produce faith. Faith produces works. Faith is proven by good works.

*True Faith is Proven by Good Works **or** True Faith Produces Good Works*
Faith ⟶ ***Salvation*** ⟶ ***Works*** (which prove faith is real)

As the above illustration shows, true faith in Jesus leads to salvation. And salvation leads to good works. The order is important. Salvation does not produce[103] faith; rather, faith leads to salvation (Acts 16:31). In the same way, works do not produce salvation; works flow from salvation. Without faith there is no salvation.

---
102 This quotation was originally given by the prophet Habakkuk (2:4) and is repeated in the New Testament in Hebrews 10:38 (just two verses before Heb. 11) and Romans 1:17 and Galatians 3:11. It is used both to describe how a person is saved and how a saved person is to live – it is all by faith.
103 The word "produce," as used here, means to "make" something or to cause something to happen.

Without salvation there are no good works.

A person has to be saved in order to produce good works. God does not accept works from a person who is not saved. Imagine if someone came to you with hands that were covered in sores and blood and holding rotten garbage full of maggots. Pretty disgusting, right? Now if that same person picked up some rice with his hands and offered it to you, would you want to take it? No, because he is coming to you with filthy hands. When an unsaved person does something he thinks is good, God does not accept it because it is offered with a heart that is filthy.[104] Our problem is doubled because not only do we have filthy hands and hearts, but we have no way to clean them! Nothing we can do will ever take away the stain of sin. But when we come to God in faith, believing in His Son, the Lord Jesus Christ, then God takes away the stain and the guilt of sin and gives us a clean heart.[105] Only then will God accept our works.

> *We can only do good works because*
> *He is at work in us.*

In fact, it is God who *causes* believers to do His will. God prophesied through Ezekiel, *"I will put my spirit within you, and **cause you** to walk in my statutes, and ye shall keep my judgments, and do them"* (Ezekiel

---

[104] See for example the Lord's explanation to Israel for why He refused to accept their sacrifices in Isaiah 1:11-15.
[105] Isaiah 1:18; Ezekiel 36:26-27; 2 Corinthians 3:3, 5:17; 1 John 3:5.

36:27, emphasis added).[106] This does not mean that God is making us do good works—as if against our will. Instead, it means that God is actively working in believers to bring about His will. Our part is to obey, to yield ourselves to God, and to seek to do those things which please Him. We can only do good works because He is at work in us. But we *can* do good works and *should* do what pleases God for the same reason: because He is at work in us. As we present our bodies to God as living sacrifices (Romans 12:1), as we present ourselves as *"instruments of righteousness"* (Romans 6:13, 16-18, 22), and as we *"seek first the kingdom of God and His righteousness"* (Matthew 6:33), we prove that we have new life and that God is at work in us.[107] God continues His faithful working in us all of our lives. He never gives up on us (Philippians 1:6).

BUT WHAT ABOUT SIN?

But what if a person does not live in a way that pleases God? What if someone says, "I belong to the Lord," but then lives like he belongs to the world instead? What if someone's life is not marked by good works? What if the direction of a person's life is toward sin and not toward God? Do you think that person has really had his life changed and made new by God? The Bible answers "No!" Someone who is truly saved *will* seek to do those things which please God. He or she will not always be successful because there is no one who is without sin. But a life without

---

106 Also see Philippians 2:12-13 and Hebrews 13:20-21.
107 See 1 John 2:29 and 3:7.

works is also a life without Christ. A fire without heat or light is a dead fire. A faith without works, says James, is a dead faith.[108]

DO PAUL AND JAMES SAY DIFFERENT THINGS?

Some people think there is a contradiction[109] between what Paul teaches and what James teaches regarding faith, but that is not the case. First of all, we need to remember that the Bible is the Word of God, not the word of Paul, or James, or any other men (2 Peter 1:20-21; 2 Timothy 3:16).[110] God's Word is perfect, without any error or contradiction.[111] Therefore, there is no real problem or conflict between what we read from the letters of Paul and what we read from James.

Secondly, at first glance there does *seem* to be a contradiction between Paul and James, but as we look closely at what they *mean*

---

108 See James 2:14-26 and especially verses 17, 20 and 26 where James makes this point.

109 "Contradiction" means there are two ideas or statements which are the opposite of each other, or that one denies the truth of the other. For example, to say "2+2=4" and also "2+2=5" is a contradiction because only one of these is true – they cannot both be true at the same time. "Contradiction" refers to things which are contrary.

110 For the sake of identifying who the human author was we often refer to a passage by saying "Paul wrote" or "Luke said" or similar expressions. However, we always need to keep in mind that the true Author is God and He used faithful men to faithfully record His exact words. They were the instruments, but God was the Author.

111 This is a major theme of the Bible and of great importance. We are not able to fully cover this topic here, but the reader is referred to these passages as a starting point: Psalm 19:7-11; all of Psalm 119; 1 Corinthians 2:13; 2 Timothy 3:15-17; Hebrews 4:12 and John 17:17.

by what they say it becomes clear they actually perfectly agree with one another. They are talking about the same thing (salvation), but they are looking at it from different angles. It is like two people talking about the sun. One person says the sun rises every day in this direction. The other person says the sun sets every day in the opposite direction. Are those two explanations opposed to each other? Does one contradict the other? No – they are both talking about the same thing (the sun), but they are talking about different times of the day and what they observe the sun doing.

What Paul Said

Paul wrote that *"a man is justified by faith without the deeds of the law"* (Romans 3:28), and that *"by grace are ye saved through faith; and that not of yourselves: it is the gift of God: ⁹ **Not of works**, lest any man should boast"* (Ephesians 2:8-9, emphasis added). Thus he makes it pretty clear that we are justified by faith and not by works.

What James Said

James, however, wrote, *"Ye see then how that **by works a man is justified**, and not by faith only"* (James 2:24, emphasis added). Twice in the same passage James says that *"faith without works is dead"* (James 2:20 and 26). That *does* seem to be quite different from what Paul said! What are we to think of this? God led both Paul and James to write exactly what they wrote. God does not make mistakes. As we prayerfully and carefully look at these passages in their contexts[112] we see that Paul and James were not in conflict; they were in harmony.

James 2:14-26 is the main passage in which James discusses the relationship of faith and works. It helps us, however, to go back briefly to James 1 to make a few notes about James' message leading up to chapter 2. There we find several good clues:

1) James warned against a false, or half-hearted faith (1:6), and said that *"a double minded man is unstable in all his way"* (James 1:8).

2) James reminds his readers that *"every good gift and every perfect gift is from above"* (1:17) and is given by the Father. Since James includes "every gift" he must also mean the gift of salvation.[113] Remember, since salvation is a *gift* it is not something we earn or work for.

3) In this same verse James tells us that God never changes, not even in the least amount.[114] This is an important point since some might suggest that God had changed His mind about faith and works, which is a thought that is neither worthy of God or possi-

---

112 The "context" refers mainly to the verses which come before and after a passage as well as the overall idea(s) the author is communicating in that particular section, chapter and book.
113 Romans 4:1-4; 6:23; Ephesians 2:8.
114 James 1:17, and see also Malachi 3:6. This is called the "immutability" of God, meaning that God does not change and cannot change. Since God is perfect as He is, any change would make Him less than perfect. God also never changes His mind since He is all-knowing at all times.

ble for God.

4) James then instructs his readers to be *"doers of the word, and not hearers only, deceiving your own selves"* (James 1:22-25). In other words, if you are not *doing* (obeying, following) God's Word, then you are deceiving yourself! You do not have saving faith if you are not obedient to what God says. Or, as James says in the next chapter, if you do not have works then you do not have true faith.

> *James said that we should be "doers of the word, and not hearers only"*

With the background of James 1 in mind, we are now ready to examine James 2, especially verses 14-26. The *way* James begins this discussion is often overlooked, but it is very important. James 2:14 says, *"What does it profit* (what good is it), *my brethren, though a man **say** he hath faith, and have not works? Can faith* (meaning "that kind of faith") *save him?"* Notice that James is talking about someone who "says" he has faith, not someone who does in fact have faith. I might *say* that I am an awesome basketball player, but that doesn't mean I really *am* that good. You might say, "Let me see you play basketball." And if you did, you would soon find out that I am not very good at basketball! How would you determine if I am an awesome basketball player or not? By watching the way I play. I would have to prove it to you by what

I did, not merely by what I said. This is exactly James' point in this whole passage. The proof about a person is seen not in what he *says* but in what he *does*.

In the next section (verses 15-16) James gives an example. If a person who says he has faith sees someone in great need of food and clothing, and if he does nothing to help, then what use is that? The needy person is not helped by someone who only *says* something like "be warmed and filled." Only *doing* something would help the person. Then James applies this idea to faith. He says, *"Even so faith, if it hath not works, is dead, being alone"* (vs. 17). That kind of faith, a faith that only says something good but never does something good, is not true faith. It is dead because it is alone (meaning not accompanied by good works).

> *The proof about a person is seen not in what he says but in what he does.*

James 2:18 continues James' point by saying that the only way for someone to really *show* he or she has faith is by works, by how that person lives. If there has been a true inward change in a person, it is only proven by outward works. True faith is proven by good works.

James says that even the demons "believe" or have faith (vs 19). Does that mean that demons are saved? No! It is not enough to simply believe that God is who He says He is. The demons do not obey God. They are evil. They might even pretend to be righteous,[115] but they tremble because they know all of their pretending will not save them. Humans who pretend to be righteous are even worse because they do not have the godly fear demons have. So James concludes that *"faith without works is dead"* (vs. 20). Notice carefully though how and to whom James says this: *"But wilt thou know, O **vain** man, that faith without works is dead?"* (James 2:20, emphasis added). The word "vain" means "empty," and in this verse refers to someone who foolishly thinks their empty (fake) faith is enough. James warns such a person that *"faith without works is dead."* If a person has true faith (meaning it is not vain or empty) he or she will have good works as a result of that faith.

True faith is proven by good works.

The hardest verse to deal with is James 2:24, which says, *"Ye see then how that by works a man is justified, and not by faith only."* Actually, this verse only presents a problem 1) if it is not seen in the entire context of what James has been saying, and 2) if only part of the verse is considered instead of the whole verse.[116]

---

115 See 2 Corinthians 11:14-15. Satan and demons act as if they are righteous in order to fool people into following the wrong thing. Many cults are based on a measure of truth mixed with deadly error, guided by the enemy.
116 Another important issue is the agreement of the rest of the Bible. Comparing Scripture with Scripture is a great help in deciding what any given passage may or may not mean. Ask, "What does the rest of the Bible say about this?"

James has been talking about the *kind* of faith a person has.[117] He has made the point that the kind of faith that does not lead to good works is not true faith. And the kind of faith that produces good works is proven to be true *by* those good works.

> *The key to understanding James' point is found in the word "only."*

James is saying something more than *"by works a man is justified"* in this verse. When we read on to the end of the verse we see James' main point. When we look at it as one piece we see what James was focusing on: *"Ye see then how that by works a man is justified, and not by faith **only**."* The key to understanding James' point is found in the word "only." This was his same point back in verse 17 when James talked about faith being "alone" (without the works that prove it is real). Good works do not *make* a person justified; good works *show* that a person has been justified. Faith, if it is true faith in Jesus, results in salvation. Salvation, if it is real, results in good works. On this point, both Paul and James and the rest of the New Testament all agree.

Let's consider once again the simple diagram from earlier in this chapter. This time we will change it just a bit by adding numbers to each part for discussion purposes.

---

117 That is why James begins this verse with, "You see then..." This verse is a conclusion based on the previous 9 verses.

Faith ⟶ *Salvation* ⟶ *Works* (which prove faith is real)

As we said earlier, this diagram is meant to show that faith leads to salvation and that salvation leads to works. Both Paul and James were describing what this diagram shows. But Paul was emphasizing the first part of the diagram: that faith (#1) leads to salvation (#2). James, however, was emphasizing how works (#3) was the result of the kind of faith (#1) that leads to salvation (#2). Or, we might say, 1+2 = 3. Paul was talking about the beginning of this process and James was talking about the end of this process, but they were both talking about the *same* process.

By God's grace we are saved by faith alone in Christ alone. But that kind of faith will not be alone. That is, true faith in Christ *will* lead to the kind of life which is marked by good works to the glory of God.[118]

> *True faith in Christ will lead to the kind of life which is marked by good works to the glory of God.*

---

[118] For more passages from the Bible which confirm this conclusion see also 1 John 1:4-10; 2:3-4; Hebrews 5:9; Romans 6 (the whole chapter); Titus 2:14; Matthew 7:17-27; Mark 8:34; John 10:27-28; John 14:15; 15:1-8.

STUDY QUESTIONS FOR CHAPTER 6

1. Romans 3:28 gives a conclusion to Paul's discussion about salvation. What does Paul say in that verse about the relation of faith and works to salvation?

2. In Romans 4, Paul describes what Abraham learned about faith and works in relation to salvation. Give a summary of what Abraham learned.

3. Explain this statement: *We are not saved **by** good works; we are saved **for** good works.*

4. Was the sacrifice of Jesus good enough to satisfy the righteous judgement of God?

5. Explain this statement: *True faith is proven by good works*

6. How does this diagram help us understand both Paul and James on faith and works?

Faith ⟶ *Salvation* ⟶ *Works* (which prove faith is real)

Chapter 7

Assurance of Salvation

HOW CAN I BE SURE OF MY SALVATION TODAY AND FOREVER?

The word "assurance" means being "sure" or "certain" of something. For example, I am sure the sun will rise in the east tomorrow. I can "assure" you of that fact because I am "sure" of it. Used this way, the word "assure" is like a guarantee. Also, I could say I have "assurance" (in this case meaning I am certain of it) that the sun will rise in the east tomorrow. Why do you and I have this assurance? Because, for every day that we have lived, the sun has risen in the east. There is no reason to believe it will be any different tomorrow.

This same word, assurance, is used to talk about our salvation. Assurance of salvation means a person is "sure" that he or she is saved. That person is also sure that he or she will be saved tomorrow, and the day after tomorrow, and forever.

How can people know for certain that they are saved now and forever? The quick answer is *"because God guarantees it in His*

Word." Jesus Christ paid the full penalty for our sin. Our salvation is not based on what we have done to earn it.[119] When we come to Christ in faith we have new life given to us and the Spirit of God living in us. God promises to never give up on us and to continue to work in us (Philippians 1:6). God makes sure that we will make it home to heaven.

This does not mean, however, that every person who says, "I believe in Jesus" can or should have assurance of salvation. It is possible for someone to say the right thing without having true faith. As we saw in the previous chapter, the true test of real faith is proven by how a person lives, not merely by what the person says.

We need to ask two very important questions. The biblical answer to these questions will guide us into thinking correctly about our assurance of salvation.

The first question to ask is: "Are people saved by what they *do*, or by faith in Christ?" The second question is: "Are people *kept* safe (or "saved") by what they do, or by faith in Christ?" As we can see, these two questions are closely related. And that is the very conclusion the Apostle Paul led the Galatians to when he wrote to them about their salvation.

*Are people saved by what they do,
or by faith in Christ?*

---

[119] See chapter 6 and also Paul's explanation in Galatians 3.

In the first chapter of Galatians, Paul reminded the readers of God's salvation by grace (not by works) which was offered to mankind based on the Savior, Jesus Christ, *"Who gave himself for our sins, that he might deliver us from this present evil world, according to the will of God and our Father"* (Galatians 1:4). Then Paul warned them about leaving the gospel of the grace of Christ[120] to accept a different kind of "gospel," which was really a mixed up and messed up version of the gospel.[121] Some people were trying to add the requirement of keeping the Law. The true gospel message is that by God's grace we are saved through faith in Christ.

Paul then went on in the next chapter to say: *"Knowing that a man is **not justified by the works** of the law, **but by the faith of Jesus Christ**, even we have believed in Jesus Christ, that we might be **justified by the faith of Christ**, and **not by the works of the law**: for by the works of the law shall no flesh be justified"* (Galatians 2:16). It is hard to be any clearer than that! Certainly, as we also saw in the previous chapter of this book, salvation comes through faith in Christ and not by our works. No amount of "keeping the Law" could ever earn salvation.

Now we come to our second question. Since we have been saved by faith in Christ, are we *kept* saved by faith in Christ, or is it

---

120 Galatians 1:6. Notice that Paul does not say in this verse that it is simply "the gospel of Christ." He calls it "the grace of Christ" to emphasize that we are saved by grace and not by works.

121 See Galatians 1:7. Paul says this would "pervert" the true gospel. To "pervert" means "to turn around" or "to distort."

by our works? That is, can we be sure we will be saved tomorrow and all the tomorrows after that? What is that "assurance" based on?

In Galatians 3, Paul said they were "foolish" to think that they could keep themselves saved by their works. He told them that just as *being* saved was based on faith in Christ, so *staying* saved was based on faith in Christ.[122] In other words, we could not earn our salvation and neither can we earn *keeping* our salvation. Salvation never came by the works we do. Staying saved is never based on the works we do. Only the work of Christ could satisfy the righteous judgment of God.

Actually, *if* our staying saved was based on our works, none of us would stay saved! This is because we all continue to sin.[123] Our staying saved is based on the finished work of Christ and the sure promises of God.

> *If our staying saved was based on our works, none of us would stay saved!*

THE PROMISE OF GOD:
BELIEVERS ARE SAVED FOR ETERNITY

If a man promises you something, your level of trust in his promise will depend on his character. If he does not have a good

---

[122] See especially verses 1-5.
[123] 1 John 1:8-10. This does not mean, of course, that it is ok to sin (see 1 John 1:4-7).

character, (if he is known to break his promise, if he is not trustworthy), then you will not have much trust in what he says. But if the man is of good character, (he keeps his promise and is very trustworthy), then you are much more likely to trust his promise.

Only God is perfect. Because of His character and attributes we can fully trust His perfect word. God is holy. God is love. God is completely faithful and true. God knows all things. God is all-powerful. God rules over all things, time, people, and all creation. God never fails. God is eternal and God is always with us. The promises of God are sure and unfailing. God's Word is without any error. We can safely and fully trust in what God says, and God says that believers have eternal life which they can never lose. Believers are saved forever. We have God's Word on it.

JOHN 3:15-16

One of the most well-known verses in all the Bible is John 3:16. Let's consider what it says along with the verse that comes before it. *"That whosoever believeth in him should not perish, but have eternal life. ¹⁶ For God so loved the world, that he gave his only begotten Son, that whosoever believeth in him should not perish, but have everlasting life"* (John 3:15-16). We notice that in both of these verses a promise is repeated for whoever believes. The promise given here is specifically that those who believe will have "eternal" or "everlasting" life.[124]

124 The Greek word "eternal" in verse 15 is the exact same as "everlasting" in

If something is "everlasting," that means it lasts forever. There is no end to what is eternal or everlasting. For a believer to "have" this everlasting life means it is both a present and a permanent possession.[125] The believer "has" or possesses everlasting life *right now* and, because it is everlasting, that life will never end. In other words, believers can have assurance of salvation (eternal life with God) now and forever.

JOHN 5:24

Jesus gives us a wonderful promise in John 5:24. He relates our assurance of salvation to the past, to the present, and then to the future in this one verse. Jesus said, *"Verily, verily, I say unto you, He that hears my word, and believes on him that sent me,* **hath** *everlasting life, and* **shall not come** *into condemnation; but* **is passed** *from death unto life."* We will view this verse one phrase at a time in order to highlight each of these "time" related promises.

PRESENT

Present time: First of all, Jesus says that whoever hears and believes **has** (right now in the present) as a possession *eternal life*. A

---

verse 16. These are just two ways of saying the same thing. Also see verse 36 and John 4:14.

125 The word translated "have" in both verses is in the present tense. This is not just a promise of what a believer will have sometime in the future, but rather a promise for the present (right now, today) that never ends (everlasting).

believer can, and should, have assurance of salvation – that their salvation will never end – right now.

FUTURE

Future time: Second, Jesus goes on to say that those same believers *"**shall not come** into condemnation."* This is a promise regarding the future. Some people may think, "I am saved today, but how do I know I will be saved in the future?" We can be sure because Jesus promises it. Remember that our salvation is based on what Jesus has already done. It is paid for completely. Jesus here promises that in the future believers "shall not" be condemned for their sins. Jesus can promise this because He took the condemnation[126] of their sins upon Himself when He died on the cross (2 Corinthians 5:21). We can be sure we will continue to have eternal life because we will never come into judgment (condemnation) for our sins.

PAST

Past time: Finally, Jesus says this promise was accomplished in the past: *"but **is passed** from death unto life."* The words "is passed" in more modern English means "has passed." This is talking about something that happened in the past and continues to be true now.[127] The thing that happened to believers in the past is

---

126 The word "condemnation" means judgment. Believers will never be condemned because Jesus was (Romans 8:1).
127 The verb is in the "perfect" tense.

that they have "passed from," or "moved from," being spiritually dead to being spiritually alive ("from death unto life"). This is referring to the moment of salvation. From that point in time, when we were saved, and going forward in time into eternity, an everlasting change took place: we moved forever from death to eternal life. That will never change!

The Three Promises of John 5:24

Passed from death to life – has eternal life_ - shall not come into condemnation

Past   *Present*   *Future*

JOHN 6:35-51

We don't have enough space here to completely cover this powerful passage, so we will simply point out a few of the main points along the way. It would be beneficial, however, for the reader to stop at this point and read this entire passage several times in order to become more familiar with it and to get a sense of the flow and connection of ideas it contains.

In this John 6 passage, Jesus again speaks a number of times about the never ending, everlasting, eternal nature of the life He provides.[128] As we have seen, since the spiritual life Jesus gives is eternal, it can never end and it can never be lost.

---

[128] See, for example, what Jesus says in verses 35, 40, 47, 51, 54, 58.

In addition to the "eternal" nature of our salvation, we also find an even stronger argument for our assurance of salvation: the sovereign plan of God. The word "sovereign" or "sovereignty" refers to the absolute, complete rule of God over all things and all times. A "sovereign" is another name for a "king." God is in charge of all things and in control of all things. God has a perfect plan which will be perfectly worked out in His exact timing and in His exact way. God is sovereign over all, meaning God absolutely rules over all. This includes our salvation.

If the reason for our salvation was because of our plan or our doing, we would have great reason to fear losing our salvation. But the plan of salvation and the work of salvation belong to God alone. As Paul told the Thessalonians, *"God hath **from the beginning chosen you to salvation** through sanctification of the Spirit and belief of the truth"* (2 Thessalonians 2:13, emphasis added).[129] The Lord Jesus, in John 6, talks about God's sovereign plan for our salvation. In John 6, Jesus tells us that 1) The Father has "given" believers to the Son, 2) The Father draws people to come[130] to the Son and believe on Him, and 3) The Son guards or "keeps" every person (without losing even one) that the Father gives to Him for eternity. God rules over the whole process and guarantees the end result; therefore, we can be sure of our salvation forever. Here are

---

[129] Also see Ephesians 1:4-6 and Romans 8:28-30.
[130] In fact, without the "drawing" of the Father, by which He calls us to Himself, none of us would come to Jesus at all (see verses 44 and 65).

a few select verses from that passage:

> ***All*** *that the Father gives me **shall come** to me; and him that comes to me I will in no wise cast out. ³⁸ For I came down from heaven, not to do mine own will, but the will of him that sent me. ³⁹ And this is **the Father's will** which has sent me, that of all which he has given me I should **lose nothing**, but should raise it up again at the last day. ⁴⁰ And this is **the will of him** that sent me, that every one which sees the Son, and believes on him, may **have everlasting life**: and I will raise him up at the last day (John 6:37-40).*

Several points to notice in particular are:

1) The first verse in this section (vs. 36) makes the amazing statement about the completeness and control of God in this salvation process. Jesus says that *all* (which He also terms "every one" in verse 40) that the Father gives the Son *shall come* to Him. There are no exceptions! We are used to thinking of John 3:16 and that the Father so loved the world (including us) that He gave His Son for us. But the amazing thing is that God so loved Jesus that He gave *us* to Jesus. And every person (*all*) the Father gave to the Son *shall come* to Him.

2) Then Jesus makes several statements about "keeping" or guarding those who come to Him. Once a believer comes to Jesus, that believer can never be lost again – Jesus guarantees it. Jesus says concerning these believers who come to Him a) "I will in no wise cast out" – meaning He accepts or receives all who come to Him and He will never get rid of or "cast out" *any* of those who come to Him; b) Jesus says it is "the Father's will" that Jesus "lose nothing" (meaning no one); c) Jesus promises to raise believers up again (to eternal, resurrected life). The reason we can be so confident about our eternal salvation is because Jesus guards us and keeps us forever.

3) Jesus talks about the will of the Father for the Son in verses 37-39. He then talks about the will of the Father for people in verse 40, which is that *"everyone who…believes in Him may have everlasting life."* The Father's will for the Son is to save and keep us safe. The Father's will for those He has given to the Son is that they "believe" in Him and receive eternal life. We are forever saved by Jesus and we are eternally safe with Jesus. We have God's word on it.

JOHN 10:27-29

Jesus secures for us a salvation which cannot be taken away from us. We see Christ's tender, constant, and eternal care for us, His sheep, in John 10. We will focus on verses 27-29, which say:

"My sheep hear my voice, and I know them, and they fol-

low me: ^{28}*And I give unto them eternal life; and they shall never perish, neither shall any man pluck them out of my hand.* ^{29}*My Father, which gave them me, is greater than all; and no man is able to pluck them out of my Father's hand."*

Here are several key ideas to glean from this passage:

1) Jesus begins by showing the connection of relationship between Himself and His sheep. He says "I know them," which is talking about more than intellectual knowledge – it means to know someone in a personal relationship. This is especially important in light of passages such as Matthew 7:21-23, where Jesus says whether He "knows" a person or not determines where that person will spend eternity! Jesus "knows" those who truly believe – those who belong to Him.

2) Jesus also points out that those who have a relationship with Him *obey* Him. The statement that *"My sheep hear my voice"* reminds us of how sheep listen to (hear) the voice of the shepherd. They look to the shepherd to guide them and depend on the shepherd to show them the way they should go. Furthermore, Jesus says His sheep "follow" Him.[131] This is another indication of the willing obedience of those who belong to Jesus. To follow Jesus means to obey Jesus. It means to follow the example of Jesus in Christ-like living and sacrificial service, always honoring

---

131 Jesus' call to "follow" Him is found often in the Gospels. Just in the Gospel of Matthew alone we often find His direction to "follow Me" (Matthew 4:19; 8:22; 9:9; 10:38; 16:24; 19:21).

God. This is a vitally important point to notice, for the promise of God concerning eternal life is given only to those who truly believe. And only those who truly believe will faithfully follow the Great Shepherd. Our assurance of salvation is based on the Savior – the Shepherd of our souls – and not on our works. But we must also recognize that if we are really His sheep we will prove it by faithfully following Him. Saved sheep are faithful sheep (though not perfect sheep).

> *Saved sheep are faithful sheep*
> *(though not perfect sheep).*

3) Jesus again reminds us of the everlasting nature of the believer's relationship to Him. He says this several ways in verse 28:

a) I give unto them eternal life

b) and they shall never perish

c) neither shall any man pluck them out of my hand

Those who believe they can lose their salvation have either not read or not understood this powerful verse. Jesus reminds us that eternal life is a "gift" (not earned by what we do), and this gift is "eternal life" (it will never end; we can never lose it). Then, to reinforce this idea, Jesus promises that they *"shall never perish."* This means His sheep will always be His sheep. The life they have in Him lasts forever. Nothing and no one can ever cause them to perish! Then Jesus gives us a beautiful picture of why that is true by saying that no one (including Satan!) can ever take us out of His hand. He holds us securely and there is no power in the universe greater than His.

4) Not only does Jesus hold us securely in the palm of His hand, but so does the Father! There is no way that anything or anyone could ever pluck us out of the Father's hand.[132] We have security of salvation because we are securely held in God's all-powerful hand. Even if we let go of Him, He will never let go of us. Nothing can ever separate us from the love of God (Romans 8:28-39).

> *There is no way that anything or anyone could ever pluck us out of the Father's hand.*

So far we have limited our studies to just a few passages in the Gospel of John. There are many more passages in the other Gospel accounts and the rest of the New Testament. What we find in those verses is in complete agreement with what we have seen in the Gospel of John. ***We can have full assurance of our salvation today and that we will not lose it tomorrow. These convictions are based on several unchangeable truths:***

1) Our salvation is based on what Jesus did, not on what we do.

2) Jesus did all that was needed to save us and to keep us safe and saved in Him forever.

---

132 In case you are wondering how we could be held in Jesus' hand and in the Father's hand at the same time, Jesus goes on to say in verse 30, "I and My Father are one." To be held by one is to be held by the other also.

3) Our assurance of salvation is also based on the promises of God. He is always true and faithful.

EPHESIANS 1:13-14

In addition to the assurances we have noted above, the New Testament provides even more biblical proof for our assurance of salvation. During the time of the Gospels, the Holy Spirit had not yet come to dwell in believers. Jesus told His disciples that the Holy Spirt was "with" them but one day the Holy Spirit would be "in" them (John 14:17). Jesus told them to wait in Jerusalem for power and presence of the Holy Spirit (Acts 1:8). Then in Acts 2, during Pentecost, the Holy Spirit came upon (and in) the disciples. From that point on, all who believed in the Lord Jesus Christ were indwelt by the Holy Spirit at the moment of conversion.[133]

As we saw in the Gospel of John, both God the Father and God the Son promised and provided reasons why we can be sure of our salvation. When we come to the New Testament letters we find that God the Holy Spirit also assures us of eternal salvation. One of the clearest passages on this blessed truth is Ephesians 1:13-14:

"In whom ye also trusted, after that ye heard the word of

---

133 Every believer has the Holy Spirit living inside of them (1 Corinthians 6:19). In fact, to not have the Holy Spirit means to not belong to Christ (Romans 8:9).

truth, the gospel of your salvation: in whom also after that ye believed, ye were sealed with that Holy Spirit of promise, [14] *Which is the earnest of our inheritance until the redemption of the purchased possession, unto the praise of his glory."*

It will help us if we break this passage into smaller parts and then see how those parts relate to one another.

1) *"In whom ye also trusted, after that ye heard the word of truth, the gospel of your salvation: in whom also after that ye believed."* The "in whom" at the beginning of the verse is talking about Jesus (see vs. 12). Paul is saying that they "trusted" and "believed" (later in verse) in Jesus. Notice that their believing happened <u>after</u> they *heard the word of truth.* The message of the gospel is necessary for true belief, so Paul calls it *"the gospel of your salvation."*

2) When they believed the gospel and were saved they were also *"sealed with that Holy Spirit of promise."* The Holy Spirit *"bears witness with our spirt that we are the children of God"* (Romans 8:14). In this way, the Holy Spirit gives us an inner peace and assurance that we belong to God forever. That in itself should be more than enough security for us! But Paul is saying here in Ephesians that we have yet another reason for certainty about our secure salvation. He says we have been *"sealed"* with the *"Holy Spirit of promise."*

What does it mean to be "sealed" with (or "by") the Holy Spirit?

While living on the Micronesian island of Yap a few years ago, we were delighted one day to hear that a ship had recently brought fresh supplies to the island. We made the long trip to the store before everything was gone, and we found a treasure: canned tomatoes. We were glad to get our little treasure home and talked about our plans to use our canned tomatoes to make spaghetti sauce, something we had not had for quite a while. However, when we got home and began to open the cans, we realized that the "seal" had been broken on all the cans. The tomatoes were ruined. When food is processed and canned, it is sealed to protect the contents. If for any reason the seal is broken, the food inside will spoil easily.

The Holy Spirit "seals" us in order to protect us and to guarantee we will arrive at our destination (Heaven) without being "spoiled" or contaminated. Our spirits are guarded by, kept by, and protected by the Holy Spirit. Nothing is able to break His seal!

A more common use of the word "seal" in Paul's day would be a seal on a document, especially an official document. Let's suppose that a king wanted to send a letter to another king. How could he make sure the other king knew it was from him and not someone else? He would roll up the scroll of the document, pour hot wax where the scroll ends, and then place his signet ring into the hot wax. The unique impression left by the signet ring would guarantee that this document belonged to the king. If the other king then received the scroll *still* sealed (so the seal was not broken), then he had confidence that the document had arrived safely.

God says the Holy Spirit is our "seal," and as such He guarantees that we belong to the King. The Holy Spirit also guarantees that each believer will arrive safely and securely at the final destination – heaven.

> *God says the Holy Spirit is our "seal," and as such He guarantees that we belong to the King.*

3) *"Which is the earnest of our inheritance until the redemption of the purchased possession"* (vs 14). Finally, Paul says that this seal of the Holy Spirit is the "earnest" of our "inheritance." The "earnest" is like a down payment on a purchase. If you were going to buy a piece of land from someone else, they might want you to give something to prove, or guarantee, your desire to follow through with the purchase. If you do not complete the deal, you lose your down payment. God guarantees we will make it home to heaven. We are God's *"purchased possession."* He has given us His Holy Spirit to live in us. This serves as a guarantee by God. Nothing can break the seal He has placed on us, and nothing can overcome the power of the Spirit within us (1 John 4:4).[134]

Sometimes other words are used to describe this biblical truth of the assurance of salvation. One such word is "perseverance," which means believers will "persevere" – that is, they will "con-

---

[134] See also 2 Corinthians 5:5 and 1:22.

tinue" to be faithful to God until the end. This does not mean they will be perfect. It does not mean they will be sinless. But it does mean they *will* (by the power, faithfulness, grace, and working of God) make it home to heaven.

Another term used for assurance of salvation is "eternal security." Eternal security means that believers are forever and always (eternally) secure (held and kept by God). These ideas, of course, are very closely related. Our "eternal security" is the foundation of our "assurance of salvation." *Eternal security* refers more to the "objective" truth of Scripture and *assurance of salvation* refers more to the "subjective" truth we sense within ourselves. For example, 2+2=4 is "objective" truth. It is true no matter how we might feel about it, or whether we agree with it or not. Eternal security is a clear biblical truth. It is true no matter how we might feel about it. However, our "assurance" of salvation *does* include how we feel. It is essential to note that our "feelings" do not change the truth! We might not always "feel" saved. This is especially true when sin is involved or when we drift away from God. However, when we remember the grace, love, faithfulness and forgiveness of God and when we remember the unchanging promises of Scripture and the finished work of Christ on our behalf; when we seek God's forgiveness and His face, then we are flooded with the inner peace, the assurance, that we are forever saved.

THE BUTTERFLY

If you had never seen a caterpillar or had never heard of the remarkable changes it can go through to become a beautiful butterfly, you probably would not believe it was possible. But God has designed the lowly caterpillar to be able to one day soar in the sky. If you told the caterpillar, "You will one day fly!" he would not believe you. He has been crawling on his belly all his life. He cannot imagine such a radical change. Could God *really* change him that much? Could he one day fly? Could it be true? Maybe it sounds too good to be true; maybe he has doubts. Do the caterpillar's doubts change the truth? No.

God says that every believer is "in Christ" and is a "new creation" (2 Corinthians 5:17). God has sealed us with His Holy Spirit and He promises that we will one day fly and much more.[135] Sometimes it may be hard to believe, but that does not change the truth. God wants His children to have the inner peace that they are forever saved (assurance of salvation) *because* He has done everything necessary to guarantee it (eternal security).

Does a butterfly ever turn back into a caterpillar? No – never. The butterfly is a new creation and God will not allow it to crawl on the dirt again as an "old creation" caterpillar. This is true, not because of what the butterfly does, but because of the design of God. A butterfly simply lives as a butterfly should live. We don't

---
135 See Chapter 8 on "Glorification" for the biblical teaching on the resurrected body.

look at a butterfly and say, "That is a caterpillar." We might say, "That used to be a caterpillar, but now it is a butterfly. It has changed to now live all its life as a butterfly."

Those who have placed their trust in the Lord Jesus Christ have been forever changed. Just as a butterfly will never go back to being a caterpillar, a believer will never go back to being unsaved. This is true because of God's design – His eternal plan. We are eternally secure, and therefore we should have assurance of our salvation.

STUDY QUESTIONS FOR CHAPTER 7

1. Are people saved by what they do, or by faith in Christ?

2. Why did Paul say the Galatians were being "foolish" (see Galatians 3:1)?

3. How does John 5:24 show that believers are saved forever?
   a) Present time:

   b) Future time:

   c) Past time:

4. How does John 10:27-29 give believers assurance that they will make it to heaven?

5. How does the "sealing of the Spirit" (Ephesians 1:13-14) give us assurance of salvation?

6. How does a butterfly help illustrate our assurance of salvation?

Chapter 8

SALVATION WORDS EXPLAINED

BORN AGAIN, ADOPTION, ELECTION

Jesus said that a person must be "born again" in order to enter the kingdom of God (John 3:3-7). What does *that* mean? How can a person be born again?[136]

I still clearly remember the moment years ago when a man talked to me about being born again. I had absolutely no idea what he was talking about. It made no sense to me.

As a young man I served in the U.S. Army. I was stationed in Germany and my boss was giving me a tour of our work area. As we came back to where the offices were, another soldier asked my boss, Jack, when his birthday was. Here is how that conversation went:

Jack asked the soldier, "Do you mean my physical birthday or my spiritual birthday?"

When I heard that question I was confused, so I asked Jack,

---

[136] That was the same question the trained religious expert, Nicodemus, asked Jesus (see John 3:4 and 9). Since even Nicodemus had a hard time understanding these things, it is not surprising we would have a hard time as well.

"What do you mean by a *spiritual* birthday?"

What Jack said next was even more confusing: "I was born on this date (and he told me when) and then I was born *again* on this date (and he told me when)."

I said, "Jack, that doesn't make any sense to me. What do you mean?"

That was, of course, the exact question Jack wanted me to ask! But instead of explaining it to me, Jack asked me if I had a Bible at home.

I said that I might have a New Testament somewhere.

Jack told me, "Go home and read the Gospel of John, chapter 3, verses 1-7. When you come back to work tomorrow I will explain it to you."

So that is what I did. I went home that night, found my little New Testament (a gift from the Gideons), and searched for something Jack had called "John, chapter 3." I finally found it, and here is what I read:

What does it mean to be "born again?"

There was a man of the Pharisees, named Nicodemus, a ruler of the Jews: [2] *The same came to Jesus by night, and said unto him, Rabbi, we know that thou art a teacher come from God: for no man can do these miracles that thou doest, except God be with him.* ³ *Jesus answered and said unto him, Verily, verily, I say unto thee,* **Except a man be born again, he cannot see the kingdom of God.** ⁴ *Nicodemus said unto him, How can a man be born when he is old? Can he enter the second time into his mother's womb, and be born?* ⁵ *Jesus answered, Verily, verily, I say unto thee,* **Except a man be born of water and of the Spirit, he cannot enter into the kingdom of God.** ⁶ *That which is born of the flesh is flesh; and that which is born of the Spirit is spirit.* ⁷ *Marvel not that I said unto thee,* **Ye must be born again** (John 3:1-7, emphasis added).

There were a lot of things I did not understand about this passage. But the one thing that stood out clearly to me is that unless someone is "born again" that person cannot enter the kingdom of God – they cannot even *see* the kingdom of God!

I had a strange reaction to this statement: anger. I had been raised as a Catholic. I had attended all the classes for confirmation. I served as an altar boy. I went to church every week. Yet in all that time, no one ever told me, "You must be born again." I had learned that Jesus was the Son of God. I knew that the Bible was God's Word. And I could see that in this passage that Jesus was giving a *command*: "You **must** be born again." I was angry because no one had ever told me that! I had learned a thousand things which seemed to have little or no importance, especially compared to this. Since no one can enter the kingdom of God without being born again, I wondered how my religious teachers could have left it out of my instruction. Did they forget? Or did they not know? How could they leave out something as important as this in their teaching?

I was also confused. What did "born again" mean? I continued to read John chapter 3 and found something which helped me a great deal. Verse 8 says, *"The wind blows where it listeth[137], and thou hearest the sound thereof, but canst not tell whence it cometh, and whither it goeth: so is every one that is born of the Spirit."* And then Jesus said in verse 12, *"If I have told you earthly things, and ye believe not, how shall ye believe, if I tell you of heavenly things?"*

I thought, "It is true that I do not understand even a lot of earthly things (like where the wind comes from or goes to, or why), so how can I understand heavenly things?" I knew I needed help. I went back to work the next day, found Jack, and asked him to explain the passage to me. That was the beginning of a six month Bible study which led to my salvation. Eventually, I realized I needed even more help than Jack could give me. I needed God to open my spiritual eyes so that I could see and understand His Word. That is what I prayed for, and God graciously answered. Perhaps you are in the same situation to-

---

[137] The word "listeth" means "wishes." So this verse is saying that the wind blows wherever it wishes to blow.

day. If so, ask God to open your eyes to the truth of His Word[138] and He will.

Why does a person need to be born again? Because people are spiritually dead without Christ. A non-believer is not just spiritually sick. It is much worse than that – he is spiritually dead. Every person born into this world is born once (physically), but needs to be born again (spiritually). We have been born of flesh and need to be born again of Spirit (verse 6). Just as we could not make ourselves be born physically, so also we cannot make ourselves be born again spiritually. This rebirth must come from someone else.

> *Why does a person need to be born again? Because people are spiritually dead without Christ.*

So how does a person become born again? One of the keys to understanding this text is found in the word translated "again." That word (*anothen*) very often means "from above, from a higher place"[139] and is probably referring to heaven. We are born "earthly" by our natural parents and earth is our home. But when we are born from above, from heaven, by our Heavenly Father, heaven becomes our home. Being born "from above" must mean being born from God – God causes our new birth. In fact, Jesus is the One who came down from heaven (John 3:13) to give new and

---
138 See Psalm 119:18.
139 *Another* can mean both "again" and "from above." It is even possible that John used it in both ways here. We are born "again" – meaning a second time, and we are born "from above" – meaning by God's working. Both are true.

eternal life to all who believe in Him (verses 15-16). This view, that the new birth (being born again) must come from God and not man, is confirmed by John 1:12-13:

"But as many as received him, to them gave he power to become the sons of God, even to them that believe on his name: 13 Which were born, not of blood, nor of the will of the flesh, nor of the will of man, but of God."

According to this passage, the people who could *"become the sons of God"* were those who *"believe on his name."* It is by faith in Jesus that one is born again. How does that happen? The next verse tells us that it is *"of God"* and not by man in any way. In other words, one must be born from above in order to be born again. God the Father sent His Son, Jesus, to connect heaven to earth by means of the cross. It is Christ, and only Christ, that can provide the connection between heaven and earth.[140] This He did by means of the cross. When we believe in Him, we have new life. That is what it means to be born again.

ADOPTION

My son, Jason, and his family recently adopted a little boy named Matthew. They already had two children, but this little boy did

---
140 See John 3:13-17.

not have any parents, so they adopted him. Matthew is now fully a part of the family. They treat him just like their other children. He has been adopted into the family and he is now my grandson.

We saw at the beginning of this chapter that the way to become part of the family of God is to be born again. The New Testament also talks about being "adopted" into the family of God. We must not think of these as two different or separate ways of entering God's family. Rather, they are two different ways of expressing the same spiritual truth. None of us deserves to be in God's family. Therefore, both our spiritual birth and our adoption into God's family must come "from above" and not from man.

> *God adopts us, not because of something great we have done, but because of His great love for us.*

My son did not adopt Matthew because Matthew deserved it. That little boy did not have to take a test or prove his worth or do anything good in order to be adopted. It was because of his great need and not his great deeds that he was adopted. In the same way, God adopts us, not because of something great we have done, but because of His great love for us. We do not have to pass a test or somehow earn God's love. In fact, we have not done great things at all. Instead, we have continually sinned against God and we have been His enemies.[141] None of us deserve to be adopted into God's family.

God sent His Son to pay the price for our sins. He did this in order to *"redeem those who were under the law, that we might receive the adoption of sons"* (Galatians 4:5). Through redemption[142] we are born again and have new life in Christ. As newly born spiritual children, we are adopted into God's family. God redeemed us for this purpose: *"that we might receive the adoption of sons."* Just as a physical child is not adopted until he or she is born, we are not adopted into God's family until we have been born spiritually.

When a man is saved (born again), his sins are forgiven. This is a huge and eternal blessing in itself! But God has even more in mind for us. He also adopts us into His family so that we stand before Him not just as someone who is forgiven, but as His child. We have an eternal *loving* relationship with God. He is our loving Father forever and He counts us as His beloved children. The greatness of this truth led the Apostle John to say, *"Behold, what manner of love the Father hath bestowed upon us, that we should be called the sons of God"* (1 John 3:1). How great is the Father's love! He gave His own Son so that we might become His sons and daughters.

Because faith is required for us to be born again, it also leads to our adoption. Paul wrote, *"For ye are all the children of God by faith in Christ Jesus"* (Galatians 3:26). A person must have faith in Christ

---
141 Romans 3:9-10; 5:8, 10 and Ephesians 2:1-4.
142 Chapter 9 gives an explanation of what "redemption" means.

in order to be adopted into God's forever family. The same faith that leads to our salvation also results in our adoption.

> *God the Father gave His own Son so that*
> *we might become His sons and daughters.*

The Bible's teaching on our adoption is meant to give us great comfort, encouragement, and assurance. A wonderful passage on adoption is found in Romans 8:14-17. We will just consider a part of that passage here.

First of all, we find this statement in verse 15: *"For ye have not received the spirit of bondage again to fear; but ye have received the Spirit of adoption, whereby we cry, Abba, Father."* Our Father does not want us to live in fear, wondering whether we belong to Him or not. Instead, it is by God's Spirit (here called *"the Spirit of adoption"*) that we cry *"Abba, Father."* The word *Abba* is a very tender term of a child for his or her father. Different languages and cultures have their own expression of this idea. In English, we may say something like "Daddy," or "Papa," or some kind of term which communicates a close and loving relationship between the child and father. That is surely the meaning here in Romans 8:15 as well. God is not a cold, distant, uncaring father. He is a loving, caring Father who is both near and dear to us, as we are to Him.

We also see in this passage another reason for the assurance of our relationship as adopted children of God. Verse 16 says, *"The Spirit itself bears witness with our spirit, that we are the children of God."* According to the Jewish law, at least two witnesses were needed to establish something as being true.[143] Because we have been adopted into the family of God, the Holy Spirit joins with our own spirit to give the witness within us that we are the children of God.

ELECTION

The biblical teaching on adoption is connected several times with the truth of election. One of those passages is Ephesians 1:4-5, which tells us, *"According as he hath chosen us in him before the foundation of the world, that we should be holy and without blame before him in love: 5 Having predestinated us unto the adoption of children by Jesus Christ to himself, according to the good pleasure of his will."* Here are several observations we should make from this passage:

1. *God chose us in "him" (meaning Christ)* God never chooses someone apart from Christ. The only way to be in a relationship with God is through the Son. We are chosen in the Son. God "chose" us to belong to Him. We did not choose Him, rather He chose us. Or as John puts it, *"we love Him **because** He first loved us"* (1 John 4:19, emphasis added). We could also say "we chose Him

---

143 For example, see Deuteronomy 17:6, 19:15; Matthew 18:16; Hebrews 10:28

because He first chose us."

2. This choosing happened "before the foundation of the world." This is a remarkable statement! The choice of whether you or I would be part of God's eternal family was *not* made in the present time or according to what we did to deserve it. None of us deserves it! God, who knows all and rules over all, did not have to wait to see what kind of person we would be. He knew we would sin and not be worthy to be saved. The choice was made even before the foundation of the world.[144] Before creation happened, God had you in mind.

Another helpful passage on election is Romans 9:6-33. We will just briefly consider one verse here. In the middle of the discussion about Jacob and Esau, Paul says that Jacob was "elected" but not Esau. Why? What did Jacob do to deserve this? The answer is given in verse 11: *"(For the children being not yet born, neither having done any good or evil,* **that the purpose of God according to election might stand, not of works, but of him that calleth;)** [12] *It was said unto her, The elder shall serve the younger."* We see clearly here that the choice (election) by God was *not* made based on anything good or bad that Jacob or Esau had done. Why did God do it that way? Paul explains: *"that the purpose of election might stand, not of works, but of him that calleth."* The purpose of election is to prove to us

---

144 See also Revelation 13:8 and 17:8 which indicate believers had their names written in the Lamb's Book of Life from before the foundation of the world.

that salvation is not based on our good works. No one ever earns salvation! Salvation is always and only based on the grace of God. Now, back to Ephesians 1:4…

3. We were chosen for a purpose, namely *"that we should be holy and without blame before Him."* God's eternal purpose for us is that we would be without any sin – that we would be holy. God knew, of course, that He would have to send His Son to die for our sins in order for us to be made holy. Because God wanted us to be with Him forever in heaven, He was willing to pay even that awful price. We could never be with Him unless we were made holy, and we could not have been made holy without the sacrificial death of Christ.

4. The next verse (5) tells us what God decided to do:

God "predestinated us unto the adoption of children by Jesus Christ to himself."

God decided beforehand (which is what "predestined" means) that we as believers would be adopted as children in His family. This is an example of how the Bible connects "adoption" with "election." Notice also that it is *"by Jesus Christ."* This is another reminder that no one is chosen apart from Christ.

5. The last phrase in this verse tells us *why* God chose us:

It was "according to the good pleasure of His will."

Verse 9 adds that it was *"according to His good pleasure which He hath purposed in Himself."* That is as far as we can see into the mystery of God's choice. It is not based on us or anything we do. His choice is based solely and completely on *"the good pleasure of His will."* God does not explain it any further than that. It pleased Him to choose us. It was His will. The only other hint we get from this or any other passage is that His choice is for His glory. The phrase *"to the praise of His glory,"* is repeated three times in Ephesians 1 (vs 6, 12, and 14). God chose us before the foundation of the world, by His own will and for His glory.

The word "election" and the words about "choice" (chose, chosen, etc.) are related. Think of it as voting for a political candidate. We make a *choice* of which candidate to vote for. If that candidate gets enough votes he will be *elected*. The people have made a choice. The result is that they chose him to be elected to the office for which he was running. In eternity past, before the foundation of the world, God had an election in heaven. There is only one God and so there was only one vote. If you are a believer, then you know He chose to elect you to be His child forever. You have been elected. God knew that one day He would send His Son, Jesus, to die for your sins. And God knew that one day He would call you to Himself, open your spiritual eyes to see, and by His grace give you the faith to believe in Him. God knew that you would believe and become part of His family forever.

The New Testament often talks about believers in terms of

the election or choosing of God.[145] As we have seen with Ephesians 1:4-5, the term "predestination" is also closely related to the election and choice of God. In fact, it is hard to think of one of these terms without the others. We have been predestined to be chosen. If you were on your way to a store you might decide before (predestine) what you would choose when you got there. God, who knows the end from the beginning, decided before the foundation of the world to choose you to salvation. What a marvelous and glorious truth! How amazing is the grace of God!

Being chosen or elected by God to salvation leads us to love and serve Him with grateful hearts. We are expected by God, and enabled by God, to live our lives in a way that pleases Him and blesses others. Here, for example, is what Paul wrote to the Colossians: *"Put on therefore, as the elect of God, holy and beloved, bowels of mercies, kindness, humbleness of mind, meekness, longsuffering; ⁱ³ Forbearing one another, and forgiving one another, if any man have a quarrel against any: even as Christ forgave you, so also do ye"* (Colossians 3:12-13). Because we are so greatly loved by God, we should love others. Because we have been so greatly forgiven by God, we should forgive others just as He forgave us. We should live as "holy and beloved" children of God.

---

145 See, for example, Romans 8:23, 11:7; Colossians 3:12; 2 Timothy 2:10; 1 Peter 1:2; 2 Thessalonians 2:13; Ephesians 1:4; John 15:16,19.

God, who knows the end from the beginning, decided before the foundation of the world to choose you to salvation. What a marvelous and glorious truth!

ELECTION AND EVANGELISM

A serious question about election that often comes up is this: "Since God has already decided (elected) all those who will be saved, then why bother to share the gospel? Won't they be saved anyway?" Here are a few answers:

1. Everything we do is for the glory of God (1 Corinthians 10:31). The reason for sharing the gospel is to glorify God. That must be our highest reason, our greatest motivation. If we put anything before the glory of God – if we think of anything as having a higher importance than the glory of God – then we will run the risk of changing the pure message of the gospel to fit what men want to hear.[146] But if you share the great news of the gospel of Jesus Christ with someone, even if that person never comes to saving faith, you have glorified God. Why do we tell people about God and salvation? The greatest reason is this: the glory of God. If that was the only reason, it would be enough.

Why do we tell people about God and salvation? The greatest reason is this: the glory of God.

---

146 This is what Paul is referring to in Galatians 1:6-10 and 2 Timothy 4:1-5.

2. When Jesus gave the Great Commission (Matthew 28:19-20), He began by declaring His authority over heaven and earth (verse 18). Since Jesus has *all authority* over all creation, our only correct response to Him is obedience. Then, Jesus gave the command to go and teach (make disciples of) all nations. This is not a suggestion: it is a command. Again, the only correct response is obedience. Why should we share the gospel? Because when we do we are being obedient to the Lord of our life, indeed, to the Lord of all. Our glad submission to our great Lord and Savior is reason enough to share the good news of salvation.

> *Why should we share the gospel?*
> *Because when we do we are being*
> *obedient to the Lord of our life!*

3. Every believer is called to be a minister of the gospel. Paul said that we have this treasure (the gospel) in these earthen vessels (our bodies). The reason God would entrust such a great treasure to mere humans is explained in the next phrase of this verse: *"That the excellency of the power may be of God, and not of us"* (2 Corinthians 4:7). God allows us this huge privilege of proclaiming His gospel in order to show His power in us and through us.

4. In the next chapter (2 Corinthians 5), Paul says that it is *"the love* *of Christ"* (vs. 14) which constrains[147] us to share the love and message of Christ with others. By *"the love of Christ"* Paul means the love which Christ has for us. Our Savior's great love for us is what motivates us to want to tell others about Him. This is true whether they will believe it or not.

5. Paul goes on to say in this passage that God has *"given to us the ministry of reconciliation"* (verse 18), and has committed to us *"the word of reconciliation"* (verse 19). Unsaved people are at war with God and are His enemies (see Romans 5:8-10). They need the peace of God and they need peace with God. In short, they need to be reconciled[148] to God. We have the privilege of telling them that because of God's amazing grace and love they can be reconciled to God.[149]

> *Our Saviors great love for us is what motivates us to want to tell others about Him.*

---

147 "Constrain" means to compel or control. It is like squeezing toothpaste out of a tube – when you squeeze the tube the toothpaste is "constrained" or caused to come out. The love of Christ is what drives us, or causes us to witness. It is the driving force behind what we do.

148 The word "reconciliation" means to bring together, to fit together, to cause to agree. When used of two people who are arguing with each other, it would mean to bring an end to the argument and restore peace between them. Lost people need to be at peace with God – that is, they need to be reconciled with God.

149 Romans 5:1, "Therefore, having been justified by faith we have peace with God through our Lord Jesus Christ."

Notice that this is called *"the ministry"* of reconciliation. The word for "ministry" here is not that of pastoral ministry. It is a word for humble service.[150] This gives us a clue as to *how* we should conduct ourselves in sharing the gospel – with humble service, not acting as if we are better than others and not being judgmental of others. As someone has said, *"sharing the gospel should be like one beggar telling another beggar where to find food."*

6. Because we have this treasure of the gospel in earthen vessels, and because we have been given the ministry of reconciliation, we are called to be *"ambassadors for Christ,"* pleading with people to be *"reconciled to God"* (2 Corinthians 5:20; 6:1).

7. We have been given a wonderful opportunity to be vessels used by God[151] to bring good news to lost people. There is no joy quite like the joy of seeing someone come to know Christ. God allows us the privilege to be part of it all. We live as aliens in a foreign land because our citizenship is in heaven (Philippians 3:20). We come telling people who are trapped in the kingdom of darkness[152] that there is another, greater kingdom, the Kingdom of Light, and the King is Jesus Christ. We come telling people who are in bondage to sin that there is freedom in Christ. How will they hear, unless

---

150 It is the word *diakonos* from which we get the word "deacon." That word was used of someone who gave humble service, and was originally used of someone who waited on tables.

151 See 2 Timothy 2:20-26 on being a vessel "fit for the master's use."

152 See Colossians 1:13; 1 Peter 2:9; Ephesians 5:8, 11.

faithful believers tell them?[153]

We have the treasure of the gospel in earthen vessels – clay pots
That all the glory may be to God

---

153 Romans 10:13-15.

STUDY QUESTIONS FOR CHAPTER 8

1. Why do people need to be "born again"?

2. *How* does a person become born again?

3. What do Galatians 4:5 and Romans 8:15-16 tell us about our "adoption" into God's family?

4. God's "election" of believers means that He "chose" them.
   a) According to Ephesians 1:4-5, *when* did God chose or elect believers?

b) What spiritual truth do we learn from the *timing* of God's election?

5. What do Ephesians 1:5 and 1:9 tell us about *why* God chose us?

6. What is the greatest reason to tell people about God and salvation?

7. God has given to believers *"the ministry of reconciliation"* (2 Corinthians 5:18-19).

How does that guide our understanding of evangelism?

Chapter 9
SALVATION WORDS EXPLAINED

REDEMPTION, PROPITIATION, JUSTIFICATION

You don't have to understand how the digestive system in your body works in order to enjoy eating a good meal of fresh fish and rice. You don't have to know all the names of all the parts of an engine in order to ride in a boat or car or airplane. And you don't have to know all the big theological words about salvation to be saved. You just need to know Jesus.

Salvation is so simple that even a child can understand and believe. Salvation is so complicated that the best and smartest theologians cannot fully understand it. Our great and wise God designed it that way on purpose.

Many people have found that the more they try to understand *how* God saved them, the more fascinated they have become with salvation. More importantly, it helps us appreciate the gift of salvation even more and worship the Savior in a deeper way. ***The purpose of theology is not knowledge; it is worship.*** No, we don't have to understand these words to be saved. But that doesn't mean they are not important. They are important to God (it is *His* plan!) and we hope, as you read this chapter, they will become important to you as well.

> *The purpose of theology is not knowledge; it is worship.*

Redemption

The first word we will consider is *redemption*. This word is used to talk about Jesus paying for our sins when He died on the cross. He *redeemed* us. But what does that mean? There are two main Greek words used in the New Testament that are translated *redeem*. The first word means "to buy something (or someone) back by paying a price." Here are some examples in the Bible where this particular word is used:

*"Christ hath **redeemed** us from the curse of the law, being made a curse for us: for it is written, Cursed is every one that hangs on a tree"* (Galatians 3:13). Because of our sin, we were under "the curse of the law." Jesus paid the price (or debt) we owed for breaking God's laws. That is what is meant by *"Christ hath redeemed us."*

Another passage that uses this word is Revelation 5:9. *"And they sung a new song, saying, Thou art worthy to take the book, and to open the seals thereof: for thou wast slain, and hast **redeemed us** to God by thy blood out of every kindred, and tongue, and people, and nation."* Jesus was "slain"[154] when He was crucified. The cross is where

---
[154] "slain" means slaughtered or murdered. Jesus was murdered on the cross to pay for our sin.

the price was paid for our sins. The result of that payment is that He *redeemed us*. That price was paid "for" us. Notice also that the price was paid *"to God"* (the Father). The price is not paid to us or to Satan, but to God the Father.

Here is an old story that helps illustrate what the Bible means when it says Jesus "bought us back" (redeemed us). A young boy loved toy sailing boats. He decided to make one for himself. It took a long time and a lot of love, but finally he finished his toy boat. He made a sail out of some old cloth, and then took his boat to put it in the water to sail it. The boat worked wonderfully and the boy loved playing with his boat. He was especially fond of the boat because it was something he had made. One day when he was playing with his boat a strong current carried it out of sight. The boy ran to where he thought the boat would end up but he couldn't find it. He searched for hours. He searched until it was dark. He searched for it the next day, but he never found his boat.

One day when the boy was walking in the village, he saw *his* boat on display in a store window! He went into the store and told the man who worked there, *"That is my boat, I made it."* But the man said he had bought it from someone else and if the boy wanted that boat he would have to pay for it. The boy looked at the price and was sad because he had no money to pay for his boat. So the boy started working at whatever little jobs he could do. He saved and saved his money until one day he had enough.

He went back to the store, gave the man the money for his boat, and walked out of the store with his boat in his arms. He held his boat closely and said to it, *"You are twice mine: once because I made you and once because I bought you back!"* That is what redemption is like. God made us, but we were lost in darkness and sold into the slavery of sin. Jesus came to pay the price to buy us back. Those who believe in Him are really twice His: once because He made us and once because He bought us back.

A second Greek word used in the New Testament to talk about *redemption* means "to loose or set free" (with the idea of paying the price). We were slaves to sin and needed to be set free from its bondage.[155] One example is Titus 2:14, which, speaking of Jesus, says, *"Who gave himself for us, that he might **redeem us** from all iniquity, and purify unto himself a peculiar people, zealous of good works."* By redeeming us Jesus "set us free" *"from all iniquity"* (sin). Yet another passage (1 Peter 1:18-19) says, *"Forasmuch as ye know that ye were not **redeemed** with corruptible things, as silver and gold, from your vain conversation[156] received by tradition from your fathers; ¹⁹ But with the precious blood of Christ, as of a lamb without blemish and without spot."* Here the price paid for our redemption is said to be *"the precious blood of Christ."* Nothing else and nothing less could pay for our sins. Notice also that His sacrifice was perfect ("without

155 See for example the teaching in Romans 6:12-23.
156 The words "vain conversation" mean "useless way of living." The idea here is that the traditions they had received from their ancestors could not save them – that way of living was useless.

blemish and without spot"). This is because Jesus never sinned. Only He could make a perfect payment to "set us free" from our bondage to sin.

Redemption means that Jesus paid the price (for our sin) to set us free (from our sin).

Propitiation

The next word we will consider is *propitiation*.[157] The word *propitiation* refers to the payment or sacrifice made to satisfy God's wrath toward sin. When we sin, we not only sin against other people, but even worse we sin against holy God. Psalm 7:11 tells us that *"God is angry with the wicked every day."* John 3:36 says, *"He that believeth on the Son hath everlasting life: and he that believeth not the Son shall not see life; but the wrath of God abides[158] on him."* Romans 5:10 says that the unsaved person is an *enemy* of God!

So *how* does a sinner change from being under God's wrath to being under God's favor? How does a sinner go from being an enemy of God to being at peace with Him? This is accomplished only by *propitiation* – a payment for our sins has to be made to God, and it has to be a payment which "satisfies" God's wrath.

[157] We almost never hear the word "propitiation" outside of church or discussions on theology, so even most people who speak English as their first language are not sure what it means. Hopefully this discussion will help you better understand it.

[158] The word "abide" means to stay, continue, remain or dwell. In this verse it means that the wrath of God *stays* on those who do not believe in Jesus.

Consider the following example. Suppose an evil person killed a loved one in your family. That person is caught and brought before a judge to stand trial. The judge says that the punishment for that murderer is that he has to tell you he is sorry. Would you be satisfied with that? Do you think that would be a sufficient punishment? What would it take to satisfy you? Should the evil person decide what is "fair" punishment?

We have all sinned against God (Romans 3:10, 23). Sin must be paid for, but what shall the payment be? Who decides? Because all sin is against God, whatever payment is made must satisfy God. *Propitiation* is the Bible way of referring to the payment that satisfies God. Since God is eternal, the payment must be of eternal value. Since God is holy, the payment must also be holy. Therefore, the *propitiation* (the payment made for our sins) must do these three things: 1) it must satisfy God, 2) it must have eternal value, and 3) it must be holy. Only the sacrifice of Jesus – the eternal, holy Son of God – could ever meet those requirements. So Jesus is called our *propitiation*. Let's look at this word in the flow of the context in Romans 3:23-25. First of all, verse 23 says, *"For all have sinned, and come short of the glory of God"* (reminding us that we are all sinners). Then verse 24, *"Being justified freely by his grace through the redemption that is in Christ Jesus"* (showing that *redemption* is through Christ). Finally, verse 25 says that Jesus is the One *"whom God hath set forth to be a **propitiation** through faith in his blood, to* *declare his righteousness for the remission of sins that are past, through the forbearance of God."* Here we see that Jesus is the *propitiation* (the payment which satisfies God's wrath) for our sins. Also notice that this payment is applied to us *"through faith in his blood."* We must exercise true faith. But why say that this faith is *in his blood*? That brings up a fascinating biblical connection to this word.

In the Old Testament, one day each year the high priest would enter the holy of holies in the Temple and offer a blood sacrifice for the sins of the people.[159] The *place* where the sacrifice was placed was the lid (or "cover") on the Ark of the Covenant. The name for this lid was the *Mercy Seat*. Now, here is our connection to Jesus and His sacrifice for us: the word *propitiation* is the Greek word for the *Mercy Seat!* Jesus is not only the sacrifice for our sins, He is also the *place* where the sacrifice is made. When Jesus died on the cross He was *that place* where the sacrifice was offered, and it was *His blood* that was shed there[160] which make the payment for our sins. On the basis of this sacrifice, those who believe go from being enemies of God to having peace with God. Colossians 1:20 tells us that Jesus *"made peace through the blood of His cross."* And Romans 5:1 says, *"Therefore being justified by faith, we have peace with God through our Lord Jesus Christ."* There is no peace with

---

159 Leviticus 16 gives the explanation of this sacrifice, known as The Day of Atonement.

160 I believe that "His blood" refers to more than just blood; it refers to the whole sacrifice, including, for instance, His pain of separation from the Father for the first time in eternity. *His blood* represents the entire sacrifice.

God without the sacrifice of Christ. But all who place their faith in Jesus Christ and His sacrifice know the peace of God and know peace with God.

Justification

So far we have seen that by *redemption* Jesus paid the price for our sins, and by *propitiation* that payment was accepted by God the Father as sufficient and perfect. Now we come to the final word: *justification*, which means that God declares us to be "just" or "righteous" based on the payment for our sins by Jesus.

John 3:36 tells us, *"He that believeth on the Son hath everlasting life: and he that believeth not the Son shall not see life; but the wrath of God abides on him."*

The wrath of God falls on those who do not believe in Jesus. But for those who *do* believe, the wrath of God has already fallen on Jesus and the believer is safe. Therefore, those who believe in the Son have everlasting life. But there is even more good news. God not only forgives our sins based on what Jesus did, He also declares us to be *justified* or *righteous*. God not only takes away the negative (sin), He also gives us the positive (righteousness).

Imagine a bowl full of stinking garbage. That is what an unbelieving person's life is like to God. God not only cleans out the garbage of our life (our sin), but He also fills that bowl with heavenly gold. It isn't just an empty clean bowl. It is, from God's point of view, a clean bowl full of gold. What is that "gold"? It is the righteousness of Christ.

By *justification* God "declares"[161] us to be righteous. That does not, however, mean that we are perfect. And it does not mean that we never sin (1 John 1:8-10). We do not earn righteousness by being good. But because our sins have been covered by the blood of the Lamb (Jesus), when God looks down on us from heaven He does not see our sin – He sees the sacrificial blood of Jesus. And it is on that basis that He calls us righteous.

Here is how the Bible talks about it: *"Being **justified** freely by his grace through the **redemption** that is in Christ Jesus:* [25] *Whom God hath set forth to be a **propitiation** through faith in his blood, to declare his righteousness for the remission*[162] *of sins that are past, through the forbearance*[163] *of God" (Romans 3:24-25).* Notice that all three of our

---

161 To "declare" something to be true means to "say" (or announce, proclaim) it to be true. *Declare* also implies the idea of *authority* in the announcement. God has the authority (and He is the only One who does) to say that we are righteous, based on the completed work of Christ in saving us.

162 The word "remission" here is the Greek word *parisis,* and it means literally "to pass over."

163 The word "forbearance" means being patient with someone and being able to put up with a difficult person or situation without punishing them. God's punishment for sin fell on His Son. Even the salvation of the Old Testament believers was based, not on the blood of bulls and goats or any other offering (Hebrews 10:4, 10-14), but on the sacrifice of Christ which would happen one day in their future. God was able then to "pass over" their sins and forgive them based on what Jesus would one day do. Therefore, verse 26 goes on to say that by doing this God is both "just" and the "justifier" of those who believe in Jesus.

words from this chapter are in these two verses. Let's focus on the word *justified* in verse 24. The *"being justified"* is passive – that means we don't justify ourselves (we are not active, but passive): it is God who does it. We are also *"justified freely,"* which reminds us that it is the gift of God, not earned or purchased by us in any way. Next, we see that we are justified freely *"by his grace,"* which again reminds us that it is by God's grace alone. Finally, we see that even this grace is given *"through the redemption that is in Christ Jesus,"* which means that the <u>reason</u> we can be *justified* is only *through* (by means of) the sacrificial payment of Jesus.

Another great verse which explains *justification* is 2 Corinthians 5:21. *"For he hath made him to be sin for us, who knew no sin; that we might be made the righteousness of God in him."*

If we break this verse down into sections, it helps us see it more clearly. *"For he hath made him to be sin for us,"* means that God made *him* (Jesus) to be sin[164] for us (sinners). Then, we have the important clarification *"who knew no sin,"* to remind us that Jesus himself never sinned. The next word *"that"* tells us the purpose, which is *"that we might be made the righteousness of God in him."* God put our sin on Jesus. But God also put the righteousness of Jesus on us! We are not righteous in ourselves, but God declares us to be righteous in Christ. God not only takes away our sin, He also gives us the

---

164 Notice that this does not say that God made Jesus "to sin" (Jesus never sinned!), but that God made Jesus "to *be* sin" for us. This means that God the Father put *our* sins on God the Son.

righteousness of Christ. That's *justification*.

Here is a way to picture it: God the Son provides *redemption* for us, and at the same time He provides *propitiation* to the Father. Based on what the Son has done, which the Father accepts as the complete and holy sacrifice for our sins, the Father offers *justification* to all who believe.[165]

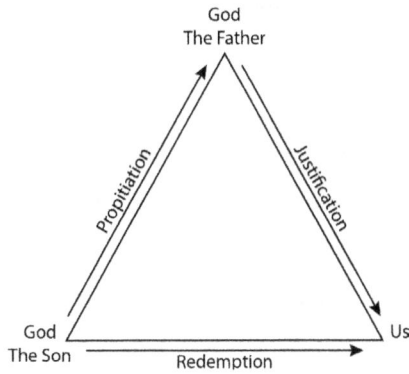

God the Son (Jesus), by being the sacrifice for our sins, does two things at the same time: 1) He provides *redemption* for us (notice the arrow points toward us), and 2) He provides the payment that satisfies the Father's wrath. That payment is called *propitiation* (notice the arrow points from The Son to the Father). Then, based on these two truths, the Father accepts the Son's sacrifice and declares us to be righteous. That is called *justification* (notice

---

165 The idea for this diagram is taken from a description by James M. Boice, *The Nature of the Atonement: Propitiation,* in *Atonement* edited by Gabriel Fluhrer, (P & R Publishing, Phillipsburg, NJ), 2010, pg. 41

the arrow points from the Father to us). In all of this we are only recipients (receivers) – that means the only thing we contribute or do is to receive. Another way to think of it is this: the *only* thing we supply to bring about our salvation is the sin which makes the sacrifice necessary! God provides for us the gift of salvation (Romans 6:23; Ephesians 2:8-9) without any work from us or worth in us. God offers us this precious gift and we receive (take) this gift by faith.[166]

Summary:

1) Jesus *redeemed* us by paying the price for our sin.

2) Jesus *propitiated* (satisfied) the Father when Jesus paid the price for our sin.

3) The Father *justified* us because of Jesus' sacrificial payment for our sin.

Here is a simple illustration which brings all three of these terms/actions together. Suppose that you and I go to a store together. I offer to buy you an item which costs $20. You and I go to the owner of the store. I pay the owner with cash. The owner looks at the money and is satisfied that it is enough to pay for the item. The owner then hands you the item, and it is now yours.

Let's think about what happened in this "transaction" or exchange. I paid the price *for* you (in your place, on your behalf), but

---

[166] Even the faith to believe is supplied by God. It is a gift from God (Ephesians 2:8). For more on *how* we receive this gift, see chapter 7.

I paid the price *to* the owner, just like Jesus paid the price *for* us and *to* the Father. The owner was satisfied that the payment was enough to pay for the item, just as the Father was satisfied that the payment Jesus made on the cross was enough to pay for our sins. The owner then gave you the item which had been purchased, just as the Father gives us salvation (declares us to be justified) based on the payment Jesus made for us. The item which has been purchased is salvation. Jesus redeemed us, Jesus propitiated the Father, and the Father justified us, and all of it is based on the payment Jesus made for us on the cross.

STUDY QUESTIONS FOR CHAPTER 9

1. The purpose of theology is not knowledge; it is _____ _____.

2. There are two main words for "redemption" in the New Testament

   a) The first word means:

   b) The second word means:

3. What was the price paid for our redemption?

4. The word "propitiation" refers to the payment or sacrifice made to _____ God's wrath toward our sin.

5. In the Old Testament, on the Day of Atonement, the high priest put the blood of the sacrifice on a special place.

   a) What was that place called?

   b) What connection is there between that place and Jesus?

6. In "justification" God _____ us to be righteous, based on the sacrifice of Jesus.

7. Draw the "triangle" illustration of redemption, propitiation and justification and label the parts. Make sure you get the arrows going in the right direction. See if you can explain these words to a friend by using the illustration.

Chapter 10
SALVATION WORDS EXPLAINED

SALVATION, SANCTIFICATION, GLORIFICATION

A lot of wrong thinking about *salvation* happens because people confuse it with *sanctification* or with *glorification*. In this chapter, we hope to make clear how these words are used to talk about different parts of what it means to be saved. Let's begin by putting them into three simple categories related to *time*: past, present and future. *Salvation* is used to refer to the past (how we became believers). *Sanctification* is used to refer to the present (how we now live and grow as believers). *Glorification* is used to refer to the future (what life will be like in the future, especially in heaven). Or, to put it another way, *salvation* talks about how we *began* the Christian life; *sanctification* talks about how we *live* the Christian life; *glorification* talks about how our Christian life *will be* in the future.

Salvation	Sanctification	Glorification
Past – how we began	***Present*** – how we now live	***Future*** – how we will be
Refers to how we became believers	Refers to how we now live as believers (includes growth)	Refers to what life for believers will be in heaven

Salvation is the beginning point. Without salvation we could never have either sanctification or glorification. In fact, without *salvation* we would not have spiritual life at all. Salvation means we have *"new life"* in Christ (Romans 6:4) because we have been *"born again"* (John 1:12-13; 3:1-7). Because salvation is the topic of this entire book and has been explained in more detail in earlier chapters, we won't take the time here to fully discuss all that is involved in salvation. But we do need to talk about it briefly so that we can show how it is different from both *sanctification* and *glorification*. If we do not have a right view of salvation, we will certainly have a wrong view of the others.

SALVATION

Even though all of us have sinned against God (Romans 3:23), God showed His great love by sending His Son (John 3:16) to die for our sins (Romans 5:8).[167] On the basis (merit) of Christ's sacrificial death, God offers the gift of salvation (Romans 6:23) to whoever believes in the Lord Jesus Christ (Romans 10:13; John 1:12; Acts 16:31). Notice that our part is simply to believe. The Son has purchased the gift of salvation for us on the cross, and the Father offers us that gift if we will receive it by faith in the Son.

We will just consider two of the important verses which teach us about salvation: Romans 6:23 and Ephesians 2:8-9.

---

[167] See the chapter on Redemption for the discussion on Christ paying for our sins.

Romans 6:23 "For the wages of sin is death; but the gift of God is eternal life through Jesus Christ our Lord."

Notice that *"the wages of sin"* is contrasted[168] with *"the gift of God."* The "wages" refers to what we earn, like when we get paid for a job – that payment is our wages. So, what we earn or deserve for *the wages of sin* (what we earn for sinning) is *death*. But *the gift* does not refer to what we earn: it refers to what we do *not* work for – something that is freely given to us even though we do not deserve it. If someone gives you a present – a gift – it is not because you worked for it; it is because someone cares for you.[169] It is the difference between a paycheck and a present. *The gift* which God gives is the opposite of death; it is *eternal life*.[170]

We notice also that this gift is given *"through Jesus Christ our Lord."* This is the only way anyone can receive the gift of salvation. There is no salvation apart from Jesus Christ. A person must put their full faith in Who Jesus is and What He has done.[171] Salvation is given through Jesus Christ our Lord. We must come to Jesus and believe in Him, not just as the Savior, but also as the Lord.[172]

168 Something is "contrasted" when it is shown to be different in some way, usually as an opposite of something else.
169 Of course, you must also accept the gift in order to benefit from it. The same is true for salvation!
170 Since the gift is eternal life, and it is contrasted with death, then the death spoken of must also be eternal. That is, this is not only talking about physical death but spiritual death (which is separation from God).
171 See the chapters on "Salvation in Jesus Christ."
172 The word "Lord" is the English translation of the Greek word Kurios in the

He is the Lord of glory (James 2:1). Jesus is Savior because He is Lord. A person cannot reject Jesus as Lord and still receive Him as Savior. And He will not be your Savior if He is not also your Lord. Otherwise, it would be like a person telling a king, "I want all the good things you can give me and your protection, but you don't have the right to tell me how to live or what to do." In other words, you would be saying, "I want to be my own king." Some people think that coming to Jesus is like that – they want His gift of salvation, but not His rule in their lives. It does not work that way. The gift of salvation is through Jesus Christ our Lord. We receive Him and we trust in Him for all He is. A word of clarification: believing in "Jesus as Lord" does not mean that we fully understand all that His lordship involves. It is a growing process. We cannot reject His lordship but we do not need to wait until we have a full understanding of it either.

Jesus is Savior because He is Lord.

Another important passage concerning salvation is Ephesians 2:8-9: *"For by grace are ye saved through faith; and that not of yourselves: it is the gift of God: ⁹ Not of works, lest any man should boast."* Here we are told that we are saved *by grace*, which is God's un-

---

New Testament. Lord refers to God as "The King." He is the Ruler and Master of all. Jesus is not only the Savior: He is the King of glory!

merited[173] favor. This removes any idea that we deserve what God has done. We also see that we are *saved through faith*. Faith is the hand that reaches out to receive the gift of salvation. Faith means to believe – not just in some hopeful way, as in, "I believe it will be a nice day tomorrow," – but in a trusting way that is sure and certain. We must exercise faith – full trust in Who Jesus is and what He has done in paying for our salvation. Next, we are told three related truths about this saving faith:

1) It is *not of yourselves*, meaning that saving faith does not originate from us; it is not something we supply. This is surprising, because many people naturally think that the faith they have is something inside them that they do. No, it isn't. The unsaved person has no faith living inside. He or she is spiritually *dead*. When they finally do have faith, it is not of themselves.

2) Also, it is *the gift of God*. God gives us the faith we need to believe! Of course, we still have to believe. God does not force us to have faith, rather He enables us to have faith.

3) Finally, it is *not of works, lest any man should boast*. The things we do, even good works, do not help us earn salvation. Our works

---

173 "Unmerited" means we did not "merit" or "deserve" what God has done. Actually, what we deserve is hell! But in God's mercy He saves us from hell, and in His grace He provides for us access to heaven instead of hell.

play no part in our salvation. Only the work of Christ – His death, burial and resurrection – is accepted as payment for our sins. Notice also that *it is not of works, lest any man should boast.* Only God deserves any credit, and He receives all the glory.

> *In salvation – only God deserves credit, and God receivers all the glory*

If you have received the gift of salvation in Christ, you are eternally saved.[174] Salvation is an event. It is something that happened in a moment in the past. Based on that past moment of salvation (when you first believed) you are now saved. But God has even more in mind for your present life, and that is:

SANCTIFICATION

Sanctification is the process[175] by which we are being made holy. It is a "process" because it is ongoing and it takes time. God grows us one step at a time. As Paul wrote, *"Being confident of this very thing, that he which hath begun a good work in you will perform it until the day of Jesus Christ."*[176] God never gives up on His children!

---

174 See chapter 6 on the Assurance of Salvation. "Eternal" refers to something that never ends. It means "everlasting" and without end. Being "eternally saved" means that salvation will never end.

175 The word "process" refers to a series of events, or steps, that lead to an end or result. For instance, when a person catches a fish or makes a meal they go through a series of steps (a process) before the fish is caught or the meal is ready. The believer grows through a series of steps, or a "process," that takes time.

176 Philippians 1:6.

He keeps working in us and with us to form us into the image of His Son (Romans 8:29). The process of our sanctification is ongoing and continual. Notice that it is also the process *"by which we are being made holy."* This is a work that God Himself is doing. The purpose of the process is to be *made holy*. The word "sanctification" comes from "sanctify," which means to "make holy" or "to be separate or set apart from sin and unto God." *Sanctification* therefore has two parts: the separation from sin (we say "no" to sin), and being set apart unto God (we say "yes" to God and His ways).[177]

> *Sanctification is the process by which we are being made holy.*

Since sanctification is a process, it has a beginning point. It starts at the moment of salvation. When Paul reminds the Corinthians of their sinful past he goes on to say, *"but ye are washed, but ye are sanctified, but ye are justified in the name of the Lord Jesus, and by the Spirit of our God"* (1 Corinthians 6:11). We see here that sanctification is connected to being justified (saved). Again, in Hebrews 10:10 we see that believers *"are sanctified through the offering of the body of Jesus Christ once for all."* In one sense, our sanctification is seen as completed in the past, based on what Christ has done for us. This is because God knows with certainty the outcome (we

---
[177] Compare with chapter 5 of this book on Receiving Salvation: Repent and Believe.

will indeed be like Christ one day) and reminds us that it is because of Christ's sacrifice for us.

The Bible also talks about sanctification as an ongoing, continual process. It not only had a beginning, but it is also an unending process of growth. When a person becomes a believer they are "born again" and have new life. But babies, both physical and spiritual, need to continue to grow and develop. When Paul reminds the Roman believers that they are no longer under the bondage of sin,[178] he then further instructs them, *"even so now yield your members servants to righteousness unto holiness"* (Romans 6:19). The word *holiness* is the same word for *sanctification*.[179]

2 Corinthians 3:18 says, *"But we all, with open face beholding as in a glass the glory of the Lord, are changed into the same image from glory to glory, even as by the Spirit of the Lord."* We are being changed into the image of *"the glory of the Lord"* and this change happens bit by bit, *"from glory to glory."* Also, this change is brought about by God. It is *"even as by the Spirit of the Lord."*

Since no believer is perfect (1 John 1:8-10), our spiritual growth is never complete in this lifetime. We are never going to be just like Christ during our earthly existence. But the goal is to become

---

178 See Romans chapter 6. This whole chapter explains the believer's freedom in Christ from the rule of sin.
179 Both words, "holy" and "sanctify," are translated from the same Greek word *hagios* in the New Testament and the same Hebrew word *qadash* in the Old Testament. If something or someone was "sanctified" that means they were "holy" or "set apart" for God and considered sacred.

more and more like Him; to continue to grow spiritually. This growth process is called *sanctification*.

God is the one who brings about our sanctification. Paul prays for believers that *"God Himself may sanctify you completely"* (1 Thessalonians 5:23). He further explains that this sanctification is through the Spirit and belief of the truth (2 Thessalonians 2:13).

But the believer also has a responsibility for their spiritual growth, their sanctification. This will require us to really apply ourselves to this growth. We need to work on our spiritual life in an active way, not just waiting for God to change us but to cooperate with Him in the process. Peter says, "And beside this, giving all diligence, add to your faith virtue; and to virtue knowledge" (2 Peter 1:5). Notice the "giving all diligence." That means to do it with all your might; to try as hard as you can. The Apostle John, talking about the return of the Lord, says "And every man that hath this hope in him purifies himself, even as he is pure" (1 John 3:3). We are to seek purity (holiness) in our personal lives. Paul says something very similar in 2 Corinthians 7:1: *"Having therefore these promises, dearly beloved, let us cleanse ourselves from all filthiness of the flesh and spirit, perfecting holiness in the fear of God."* These, and many other passages like them, tell us that we are to have an active part in seeking to grow spiritually. Remember that we do not work for our salvation – it is a free gift of God. But we do work toward our sanctification. As believers we have an active part to play in growing to be more and more like Christ. It is true that in this present life we will not be sinless, but it is also true that as we grow we should definitely sin less!

*In this life, we may not be sinless,
but we should definitely sin less!*

The Apostle Paul makes a startling statement in Philippians 2:12: *"Work out your own salvation with fear and trembling."* If that had been the end of what Paul said on this topic, we would have great reason for concern! But Paul goes on to immediately add in the context, *"For it is God which works in you both to will and to do of his good pleasure"* (Philippians 2:13). We are not left on our own. We do not have to come up with our own plan and power. God Himself is at work in us *"both to will and to do of his good pleasure."* He gives us the *will* (the desire) and He gives us the ability *to do* what pleases Him. He has provided everything we need in order to live successful spiritual lives. By His great power God has *"given us all things that pertain*[180] *unto life and godliness"* (2 Peter 1:3). We can never say to God, *"If You had just given me more _____* (fill in the blank with whatever you think you might be missing), *I would have been able to live a more righteous life."* God has given us all we need for the Christian life and for godliness.

God uses two holy things to sanctify us: the Holy Spirit and the

---
180 The word "pertain" here means "all the things that are a part of" life.

holy Bible.[181] He uses His Spirit and His Word. For instance, Paul says, *"God hath from the beginning chosen you to salvation <u>through sanctification of the Spirit</u> and belief of the truth"* (2 Thessalonians 2:13). And Jesus prayed *"Sanctify them through thy truth: thy word is truth"* (John 17:17). God supplies His Spirit and His Word, but we must participate. We must yield[182] to His Spirit and follow His Word.

If a parent provides food for his child and the child refuses to eat, the child will become weak. If we do not depend on the Spirit and eat the spiritual bread of the Word, we will become spiritually weak. To grow, we need to read the Bible, study it, mediate on it, follow it and ask God by His Spirit to enable us to both understand and obey the Bible. A believer who does that will grow and will, more importantly, glorify God.

---

181 In some ways, God also uses other believers to sanctify us, but because this happens as they teach, encourage, exhort, rebuke and admonish us according to God's Word or by God's Word, these would still fall under the heading of the Bible. That is, *people* don't sanctify us, but as people use the Bible, God uses them in our sanctification.

182 To "yield" ourselves means to "surrender" ourselves or to give ourselves completely. Used in this way it means we agree with and accept God's rule over us. We therefore agree to follow His Word and long to be led by His Spirit.

Here is a simple chart to compare salvation and sanctification:

SALVATION *Christ died for us*	SANCTIFICATION *Christ lives in us*
Refers to our Position (does not change)	Refers to our Condition (does change)
Refers to our Relationship with God	Refers to our Fellowship with God
Refers to our Peace *(Christ for us)*	Refers to our Purity *(Christ in us)*
Refers to the Past work of Christ	Refers to the Present work of Christ
By Salvation we are *declared* to be righteous	By Sanctification we are *becoming* righteous

As was mentioned at the beginning of this chapter, it helps to think of these terms in relation to *time*. For a believer, salvation refers to the *past* and how he or she became saved. Sanctification refers to the *present* and how the believer is now being changed to be more like Christ. Our final word, glorification, refers to the *future* and what the believer will be like in heaven.

We can also think of these three terms in relation to ***sin***:

SALVATION Past	SANCTIFICATION Present	GLORIFICATION Future
Frees us from the **Penalty** of Sin	Frees us from the **Power** of Sin	Frees us from the **Presence** of Sin
God forgave our sin and took away all guilt	God conquers our sin and breaks sin's power over us	God will remove every trace of sin and sin nature in us

We now turn our attention to this last word: *glorification*.

GLORIFICATION

Glorification does not happen in this life. Believers are not glorified until they are in heaven, so when we talk about glorification we are talking about something that is in the future. Actually, the final step of glorification will happen in the end times when Jesus will return to earth and raise the dead bodies of all believers from all times. Jesus will then change all of those dead bodies into perfect resurrected bodies and join them back together with their spirits.[183]

The Apostle John wrote, *"Beloved, now are we the sons of God, and it doth not yet appear what we shall be: but we know that, when he shall appear, we shall be like him; for we shall see him as he is"* (1 John 3:2). Believers are "now" children of God. In the future, when Jesus returns (*"when he shall appear"*), believers will be changed to be "like him" both spiritually and physically. That will be glory!

God deserves *all* the glory and *only* God deserves glory. Just like none of us deserves to be saved, so it is true that none of us deserves to have glory. The love of God is so great that He gave His Son to die for us. Upon this gracious gift of salvation God piles more blessings, the last of which is our glorification. In eternity

[183] The "spirit" or "soul" of a believer who has died goes immediately to be with Jesus in heaven. But the body is still here on earth. In the end times, at the final resurrection, the body is made perfect and joined back to the spirit of the believer.

to come we will have spirits and bodies which have been made perfect forever – that is glorification.

In the process of sanctification, we are being made more and more like Jesus. God continues His faithful working in us to change us into the image of His Son and our Savior. Think of sanctification as a step by step process. Each step brings us closer to Christlikeness. The final step, when we will actually be like Christ, is called *glorification*. At that time, we will be made perfect, both spiritually and physically.

Glorification means the perfecting (making perfect) of both our spirit and our body. As the final step of the sanctification process, we will finally and forever be spiritually pure. Right now, in this present life, we are "declared" righteous.[184] In the next life we will actually *be* righteous. We will be freed from temptation, sin, the old nature (sin nature) and the influence of Satan.

God continues to work on us in this life[185] to make us more like Christ. Jesus sanctifies and cleans us spiritually by *"the washing of water by the word"* (Ephesians 5:26). The Bible is the soap Jesus uses to wash us. His purpose in doing this is given in the next verse: *"That he might present it[186] to himself a glorious church, not having spot, or wrinkle, or any such thing; but that it should be holy*

---

[184] See chapter 9 under the topic of "justification" for what it means to be declared righteous.

[185] Philippians 1:6; Colossians 1:22.

[186] The "it" in this verse is referring to the Church, for which Jesus gave Himself on the cross (Ephesians 5:25).

and without blemish" (Ephesians 5:27). We are being prepared to live with Jesus forever in glory. We are being cleansed (sanctified) now, and one day we will be completely clean (glorified).

Our glorification has always been God's purpose for us. We should all reflect His glory, like the moon reflects the light of the sun, but because of our sin we are like muddy mirrors. We don't reflect God's perfect image because *"all have sinned, and come short of the glory of God"* (Romans 3:23). God's plan is to change us so that we are like Christ and perfectly reflect His image. Romans 8:29 says, *"For whom he did foreknow, he also did predestinate[187] to be conformed[188] to the image of his Son."* God has a plan, a purpose (vs 28), a destiny (vs 29) for every believer – that we will be changed into the image of His Son. That is what is meant by glorification.

> *God's plan is to change us so that we are like Christ and perfectly reflect His image.*

When we are glorified we will be like Christ.[189] The Apostle Paul goes on to explain: *"Moreover whom he did predestinate, them he also*

---

187 "Predestinate" means to determine or decide something before it happens. The first part of the word (pre) means "before." The second part (from "destine") means "to decide." God decided before the foundation of the world (Ephesians 1:4-5) to make us His children and to make us into the image of His Son. Also see chapter 8.

188 "Conformed" means to be changed. Every believer will be changed to be like Christ.

189 That does not mean we will be Christ but that we will be like Christ. Christ is God and we will never be "gods."

called: and whom he called, them he also justified: and whom he justified, them he also glorified" (Romans 8:30). God decided[190] that every person who will believe in Jesus will be called (to salvation), justified (saved), and glorified.

Notice especially that the word "glorified" is in the past tense. We are not yet glorified, so why speak of it as if it had already happened? Because God, Who knows all things and controls all things, guarantees that every believer will be glorified. He holds every believer safely and securely in His hand and will bring each one home to glory.[191] From God's point of view, our being glorified is a done deal because it is not based on us or anything we do. Instead, it is based on the completed work of Christ, the faithfulness of our Heavenly Father, and the sealing[192] of the Holy Spirit. We will be glorified, but God gets all the glory!

In addition to being made spiritually pure, glorification will also change our physical bodies. We will not be like spirits without bodies in heaven. Our bodies will be resurrected by Christ[193] and immediately changed to be perfect bodies which will live forever and be joined together again with our spirits.

---

190 Actually, a stronger word like "decreed" or "ordained" is called for. Those words more accurately communicate the idea that this "decision" by God is not changeable.

191 John 10:28-29; John 6:39-40; Ephesians 1:14.

192 The Holy Spirit lives inside of each believer and "seals" or secures them so that they are guaranteed to make it safely home to heaven (Ephesians 1:13-14).

193 See 1 Thessalonians 4:13-18 and 1 Corinthians 15:50-58.

*We will be glorified, but God
gets all the glory!*

PRESENT SUFFERING = FUTURE GLORY

In this present life we suffer physically. The bodies we currently have are not designed to last for eternity. They wear out. They suffer sicknesses and diseases of many sorts. Eventually, these bodies will die and turn to dust. But that is not the end of the story for our bodies. God will one day raise up the bodies of all believers from all times and places, and change each of those bodies into a brand new, perfect body. For now, we are eagerly awaiting "the redemption[194] of our body" (Romans 8:23).

Paul, who knew what it was like to suffer, said this: "For I reckon that the sufferings of this present time are not worthy to be compared with the glory which shall be revealed in us" (Romans 8:18). Sometimes the suffering we go through, or watch loved ones go through, can be terrible. But even the worst suffering is "not worthy to be compared" with what God has planned for us through "the glory which shall be revealed in us." Comparing our present suffering with our future glory is like comparing a bucket of water

---

[194] Our spirits have already been "redeemed" at salvation, but we still have our old bodies during this life. One day (at the resurrection) our bodies will also be redeemed and be made new.

with the ocean, or a grain of sand with a mountain. This is not to say that the present difficulties and diseases people go through are easy or mean nothing. They may be very bad indeed. But 10,000 years from now, when our eternity has just begun, those bad memories (if we remember them at all) will be in the very distant past and the glory of heaven will be our new and overwhelming reality.

A little boy in our church fell down last night. He scratched his face a bit and he hurt his arm in the fall. It hurt and he cried a lot. Let's suppose that in twenty years from today, when that little boy is a grown man, it is his wedding day. His excitement and joy over getting married to this woman he loves will so greatly overshadow the pain of that time he fell as a little boy that it will be as if it never happened. Our hurts of today will be like a drop of water swallowed up in the ocean of eternity.

> *Our hurts of today will be like a drop of water swallowed up in the ocean of eternity.*

Not only will our glorified bodies be without pain or suffering or any defects at all, but they will be that way *forever*. In that day, *"God shall wipe away all tears from their eyes; and there shall be no more death, neither sorrow, nor crying, neither shall there be any more pain: for the former things are passed away"* (Revelation 21:4).

What will our new resurrected bodies be like? Although we

cannot know the complete answer to that question, we do have some clues. For one thing, our resurrected bodies will be like Christ's resurrected body.[195] When our risen Lord appeared to His disciples after the resurrection He had a real physical body. Jesus invited the disciples to touch Him and see for themselves that *"a spirit does not have flesh and bones as you see I have"* (Luke 24:39). The resurrected body of Jesus was a real "flesh and bone" body. Jesus knew they still had a hard time believing so *"he said unto them, Have ye here any meat? ^{42} And they gave him a piece of a broiled fish, and of an honeycomb. ^{43} And he took it, and did eat before them"* (Luke 24:41). By physically eating food, Jesus was again proving to them that His body was real. So our resurrected bodies will be physical, real bodies, able to eat and drink, able to touch and to be touched. On at least two occasions[196] after His resurrection, Jesus appeared to His disciples while they were locked inside a room. He did not come through the doors, He just appeared in the room! Even though He had a physical body, He was able to pass through the solid wall! This is just one example that our resurrected new bodies will have very special abilities beyond what we can imagine now. Paul explains that Jesus will *"change our vile[197] body, that it may be fashioned like unto his glorious body"* (Philippians 3:21).

The main passage in the New Testament on what our glorified,

---
195 1 Corinthians 15:48-49; 1 John 3:2.
196 See John 20:19 and John 20:26.
197 "Vile" here means "lowly, humble" and refers to our present earthly bodies. It does not mean that our bodies are bad, just that they are not glorious.

resurrected bodies will be like is 1 Corinthians 15:35-54. From that passage (especially verses 42-49) we learn some key truths about the resurrected body:

1) The resurrected body will change from being corruptible to being incorruptible.[198] The present earthly bodies we have are "corruptible" – they get sick, injured, and old, they wear out and finally die. By contrast, the resurrected bodies of believers will *not* suffer any of those things – they will be "incorruptible" (meaning they cannot be "corrupted"). Those bodies will last forever and never have any problems. Our resurrected bodies will always be strong and healthy. Those bodies will also never get old and wear out, which raises the question of how old, or what age, our resurrected bodies will be. We cannot know for certain and we will not be thinking in terms of "time" or "age" in eternity anyway. We will be of full, mature age (so not like children), but we will not be old either, so it would make the most sense to think of our resurrected bodies as young, but mature.

2) The resurrected body will change from a state of "dishonor" to one of "glory."[199] Our bodies will be made "glorious" by Jesus. From the way the words "glory" and "glorious" are used in the Bible, this most likely means our resurrected bodies will have a beautiful appearance which will shine brightly. When Jesus was talking about the Kingdom of Heaven, he said, *"Then shall the righ-*

---
198 Verse 42 and verses 50-54.
199 Verse 43.

*teous **shine forth** as the sun in the kingdom of their Father"* (Matt. 13:43).[200]

3) The resurrected body will change from "weakness" to "power."[201] Even the strongest men on earth will seem like weak children compared to the power of any person with a resurrected body. Our "natural" bodies here on earth are weak and limited. Our resurrected bodies will have capabilities much beyond our natural abilities, and will, therefore, be in a sense "supernatural" bodies. That does not mean we will have power like God has, but it means we will have power beyond what we can imagine now.

4) The resurrected body will change from a "natural" body to a "spiritual" body.[202] Another way to think of this change is that it will be from our present *earthly* body to our future *heavenly* body. Our present bodies, made of flesh and blood and corrupted by sin, cannot enter into God's glorious presence.[203] We must have a new body which will be able to last for eternity and, more importantly, will be "spiritual"[204] so that it can be in God's holy presence.[205] God has fully supplied all this and more through salvation, sanctification and glorification.

---

200 See also Daniel 12:3, Matthew 17:2 and Exodus 34:35.
201 Verse 43.
202 1 Corinthians 15:44-49.
203 See especially 1 Corinthians 15:50.
204 "Spiritual" is used here is the sense of being in tune with the Holy Spirit. It is not a contrast to "physical," but rather it is contrasted with that which is "earthly" or "worldly."
205 Habakkuk 1:13; Revelation 21:27.

Summary:

One way of thinking about the relationship and meaning of these three words (salvation, sanctification and glorification) is to think of them in terms of a trip on an airplane.[206]

Salvation: Jesus fully paid the price for our salvation. He purchased our ticket for our trip to heaven when He died on the cross for our sins. But salvation is much more than merely getting a ticket to heaven. It means new life in Christ *now*. Not only are we born again, we are meant to *grow* as believers, a process called sanctification.

Sanctification: For all of our saved lives we are on a journey, a trip, toward heaven and glory. Just as an airplane ride may include some ups and downs, going through storms, fearful moments and enjoyable moments, our journey toward heaven will have its own ups and downs, storms of life, fearful moments and joyful moments. All of this is designed to help us grow and to prepare us for the destination ahead of us: heaven. The Holy Spirit is with us all the way and promises us that we will safely make it home.

Glorification: One day, we will finally arrive at our new heavenly home. We will see Jesus face to face, and in that moment

---

[206] No analogy is perfect, and there are issues even with this one, but our purpose is to at least set forth the general idea.

we will realize that we have been changed to be like Him.[207] That will be glory! *"And so shall we ever be with the Lord"* (1 Thessalonians 4:17).

For I am not ashamed of the gospel of Christ: for it is the power of God unto salvation to every one that believeth; to the Jew first, and also to the Greek.
[17] For therein is the righteousness of God revealed from faith to faith: as it is written, The just shall live by faith.
(Romans 1:16-17)

But we are bound to give thanks always to God for you, brethren beloved of the Lord, because God hath from the beginning chosen you to salvation through sanctification of the Spirit and belief of the truth.
(2 Thessalonians 2:13)

---

207 1 John 3:2-3.

STUDY QUESTIONS FOR CHAPTER 10

1. What does Romans 6:23 tell us about the "gift" of God?

2. Use Ephesians 2:8-9 to give a summary of how a person is saved.

3. The definition of "sanctification" is that *Sanctification is the* _____ *by which we are being made* _____.

4. Give at least two ways in which sanctification is *different* than salvation

   a)

   b)

5. How long does the sanctification process last?

6. Philippians 2:12 says to *"work out your own salvation with fear and trembling."*

   How does the next verse (13) explain how we can do that?

7. Glorification means the _____ of both our spirit and our body.

8. God's plan is to change us so that we are like _____ and perfectly reflect _____ image.

9. What will our glorified bodies be like?

www.ingramcontent.com/pod-product-compliance
Lightning Source LLC
Chambersburg PA
CBHW050535300426
44113CB00012B/2114